The Two Princes of Calabar

The Two Princes of Calabar

AN EIGHTEENTH-CENTURY
ATLANTIC ODYSSEY

Randy J. Sparks

HARVARD UNIVERSITY PRESS

Cambridge, Massachusetts
London, England

First Harvard University Press paperback edition, 2008.

Library of Congress Cataloging-in-Publication Data
Sparks, Randy J.
The two princes of Calabar : an eighteenth-century
Atlantic odyssey / Randy J. Sparks.
p. cm.
Includes bibliographical references and index.
ISBN 978-0-674-01312-4 (cloth : alk. paper)
ISBN 978-0-674-03205-7 (pbk.)
1. Blacks—England—History—18th century. 2. Antislavery
movements—Great Britain—History—18th century. 3. Slave-trade—
Great Britain—History—18th century. 4. Slavery—Great Britain—
History—18th century. 5. Slave-trade—Nigeria—History—18th century.
6. Nigerians—England—History—18th century. 7. Slavery—Nigeria—
History—18th century. 8. Robin John, Little Ephraim, fl. 1767. 9.
Robin John, Ancona Robin, fl. 1767. 10. Calabar (Nigeria)—Biography.
11. Nigeria—History—To 1851. 12. Calabar (Nigeria)—History.
13. Freedman—Biography. I. Title.
DA125.N4S66 2004
909'.049607'092266944—dc22
[B]   2003056832

For Linda S. Ferguson

Contents

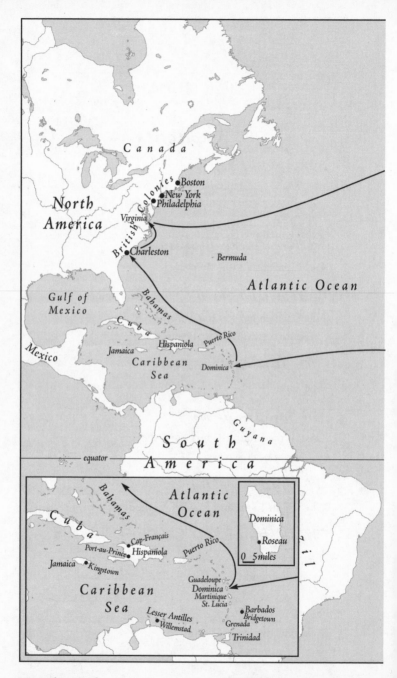

The Robin Johns' voyages around the Atlantic World

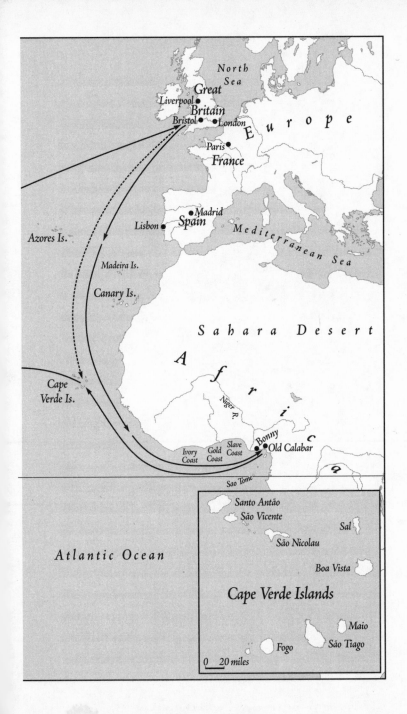

North
Sea

Great
Britain
Liverpool •
Bristol •
• London
Europe

Paris •
France

• Madrid
Lisbon •
Spain
Mediterranean Sea

Azores Is.

Madeira Is.

Canary Is.

Sahara Desert

A
f
r
i
c

Niger R.

Cape
Verde Is.

Bonny
Ivory
Coast
Gold
Coast
Slave
Coast
• Old Calabar

Sao Tome

Atlantic Ocean

Santo Antão
São Vicente
Sal
São Nicolau
Boa Vista

Cape Verde Islands

Maio
Fogo
São Tiago

0   20 miles

The Two Princes of Calabar

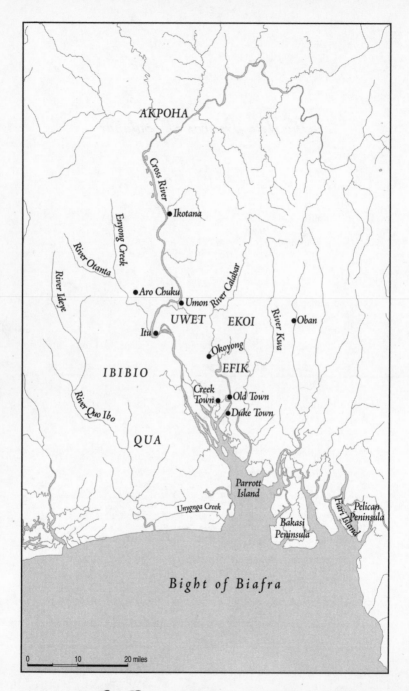

Old Calabar in the eighteenth century

Prologue

In 1767 Little Ephraim Robin John and Ancona Robin Robin John, were captured during an ambush by English slavers in the African port of Old Calabar and sold into slavery in the Americas. The young men were members of the ruling family of Old Town, a major slave-trading town in Old Calabar. Grandy King George, the ruler of Old Town, was Little Ephraim's brother and Ancona's uncle. Those relationships led the English to refer to them as princes, though "prince" was not a title in use in their native land. Their remarkable odyssey took them from Africa, to the Caribbean, to Virginia, to England, and finally back to Africa. Their story, written in their own hand, survives as an early, and as yet virtually unknown, firsthand account of an Atlantic slave experience with important implications for the history of the slave trade, slaves' relentless quest for freedom, the early British antislavery movement, and the role of enslaved Africans in the creation of the early modern Atlantic World.

Those of us engaged in historical research know well the joys of chance discoveries. This project began when I visited the John Rylands Library in Manchester, England, where I was researching a topic in the history of early nineteenth-century American and British Methodism. The Rylands Library was built in honor of John Rylands, one of England's wealthiest cotton manufacturers and merchants, whose business was closely linked to plantation slavery. As I scanned the catalogue to the papers of Charles Wesley, the brother of the founder of Methodism, John Wesley, and one of the greatest Protestant hymnodists, I ran across descriptions of a series of letters written by former slaves to Charles. Intrigued by the brief references in the catalogue to the collection, I asked to see the letters. What I found were a series of letters written to Wesley by Little Ephraim Robin John and Ancona Robin Robin John, natives of Old Calabar, a slave-trading depot on the West Coast of Africa, who were enslaved in the Americas before making their way to England. I found the letters so compelling that I began to find out as much as I could about the men and their story, a project that has led me to research in the histories of Africa, the slave trade, the Caribbean, and England.

With Columbus's voyage in 1492, the Atlantic Ocean was transformed from a barrier into a bridge, and complex links began to emerge between Europe, Africa, and the Americas. Much important work has been done on the emergence and growth of the Atlantic World in recent years, though the topic is usually taken up in broad studies that have addressed such topics as the exchange of plants, animals and diseases, the massive movement of people, the rise of new economic systems, the transfer of culture and institutions, and the development of empires.[1] But in this book I explore the impact of the rise of the Atlantic World on a particular place in time—eighteenth-century Old Calabar—through the lives of two men who were themselves products of that Atlantic World. Their identities were shaped by it and they moved through it—often touched by those large impersonal forces that have captured so much scholarly attention, and their story can provide a microhistory of the eighteenth-century Anglo-Atlantic World. The Robin Johns can best be understood as Atlantic creoles. My use of that term is borrowed from the historian Ira Berlin. In defining Atlantic creoles, Berlin is moving away from the definition of creoles as individuals of African or European origin born in the New World toward a definition that owes more to linguists and their understanding of creolized languages. In his definition, it is culture, not birth, that designates Atlantic creoles. As Berlin wrote:

Along the periphery of the Atlantic—first in Africa, then in Europe, and finally in the Americas—

African-American society was a product of the momentous meeting of Africans and Europeans and of their equally fateful encounter with the peoples of the Americas. Although the countenances of these new people of the Atlantic—Atlantic creoles—might bear the features of Africa, Europe, or the Americas in whole or in part, their beginnings, strictly speaking, were in none of those places. Instead, by their experiences and sometimes by their persons, they had become part of the three worlds that came together along the Atlantic littoral. Familiar with the commerce of the Atlantic, fluent in its new languages, and intimate with its trade and cultures, they were cosmopolitan in the fullest sense.[2]

The Robin Johns were such individuals, and their story will help bring the lives of Atlantic creoles into sharper focus.

The Atlantic slave trade was the largest forced migration in human history. Over the course of the trade, approximately eleven million men, women, and children from a wide variety of African ethnic groups were captured, sold, and transported to the New World.[3] Despite the vast scope of the trade, firsthand accounts from the victims themselves are extremely rare. Largely illiterate (though not entirely, as the example of the Robin Johns illustrates), captives had few opportunities to write down their stories, and few slave masters had any interest in their doing so. Typically they were enslaved in brutal and harsh conditions in the plantation societies of the New World, and so there was little chance that any records from the slaves themselves could survive. For decades, historians of the slave trade played the "numbers game," a long-running and often heated debate over the extent of the trade and the number people who fell victim to it. While there can be no question that the numbers are vital to a full understanding of the trade and of its terrible costs in human lives, that focus on the numbers often obscured the individual stories of those who experienced enslavement. The challenge is to translate those statistics into people. Indeed, most of those individuals are lost to history—it is now impossible to reconstruct the lives of eleven million individuals, though only that could fully reveal the scope of the trade's tragic impact. The sheer number of victims defies easy comprehension, and yet we know that great diversity of experience lies behind those numbers. The Robin Johns offer one opportunity to portray victims of the trade in greater detail and to restore the voices of two of the individuals who survived the Middle Passage, the journey from the west coast of Africa to the Americas. Their story is filled with surprises, and they cannot be considered typical of the men who were enslaved in Africa.

Perhaps the most shocking aspect to the Robin Johns' story for modern readers is that they were themselves slave traders. The slave trade spread its tentacles throughout the Atlantic World, and it could not have been conducted so successfully without the complicity of men and institutions in Europe, Africa, and the Americas. The Robin Johns must be situated within the history of their home in Old Calabar, an important trade depot located in the Bight of Biafra, one of the most intensely trafficked slave-trading regions anywhere in Africa. This area rose to prominence in the trade only in the mid-eighteenth century as families like the Robin Johns created thriving commercial trading houses in Old Calabar built on the profits from the slave trade.

In 1767 several British Guineamen, as the slave ships were called, lay in the Calabar River, where they engaged in a lucrative trade with their African counterparts, members of an ethnic group known as the Efik. That trade was dominated by a relatively small number of English slave traders in Bristol and Liverpool and Efik slave traders in Old Calabar. Those English and African merchants formed long-term relationships, nurtured through education, social interactions, and fictive kinship ties, but those relationships could be brittle and could quickly be undermined by the violence that plagued the trade. By the mid-1700s a bitter trade rivalry existed between Old Town and New Town, the largest settlements in Old Calabar. The competition between Old Town and New Town flared in 1767 when the New Town traders persuaded British ship captains to join them in entrapping and murdering several hundred residents of Old

Town involved in the trade, a pivotal event in the history of Old Calabar. During the bloody battle, a British captain captured two members of the ruling family of Old Town, Little Ephraim Robin John and Ancona Robin Robin John.

The captain carried the men to the Caribbean island of Dominica, where they were sold to a French physician. After several months, a ship's captain offered to help the young men escape to freedom. Their activities hint at the complexity that surrounds the African slave trade. These men were creolized Africans from a coastal region where close and long-standing ties between British and African merchants had enabled them to learn English and other skills useful to the members of a prominent merchant family. Their example serves as an important reminder that not all native Africans sold as slaves in the Americas fit the stereotype of the "outlandish" African, who knew nothing about European languages or culture. The Robin Johns attempted to use their considerable language and interpersonal skills to negotiate their escape. They may well have assumed that bargains such as the one they struck with the ship captain could be relied upon, as they generally could on the coast of West Africa, where slavers depended heavily on the good will of the local African elites. Rather than returning them to Africa as agreed, however, the captain sold the Robin Johns to a merchant in Virginia. After five years in Virginia, the princes met two of their countrymen from Old Calabar who had sailed to America aboard a slave ship from Bristol. The men described the princes' plight to their captain, who convinced the princes that he would return them to Old Calabar if they ran away with him. The princes escaped and boarded his ship, but the captain took them to Bristol, where he attempted to sell them into slavery once again.

Desperate to escape, the young men wrote to Thomas Jones, a Bristol merchant and slave trader, who helped get them off the ship, but they had to remain in jail until they successfully appealed to William Murray, Lord Chief Justice Mansfield, who helped free them. Their case is a significant one in the history of the legality of slavery in Britain. Their case was the first dealing with slavery in Britain following the landmark *Somerset* case, in which Mansfield ruled in 1772 that James Somerset, once enslaved in Virginia, could not be forced to return to bondage in America because slavery was not supported by English law. The Africans asked for and received spiritual instruction and reading lessons from Charles Wesley. They were frequent visitors in the Wesley household and wrote affectionate letters to Wesley and his children. They came into frequent contact with Charles's brother, John, and they were converted to Methodism and baptized. After several months in England, the princes sailed for Old Calabar, but their ship was wrecked in a storm on a deserted island off the African coast. Rescued after sixteen days by a ship bound for Bristol, they were forced to return to England. After another stay of several months, they set out again and finally made their way back to their home in Old Calabar. Once back in Africa they remained in contact with English friends and invited the first Methodist missionaries to come to Africa. The evidence indicates that they also went back to their old business as slave traders, highlighting the complexities and moral ambiguities that surround the trade.

Their remarkable story, preserved in their own hand, offers a rare glimpse into the eighteenth-century slave trade from the perspective of the Africans themselves. Recently, scholars have called into question the authenticity of the best-known eighteenth-century slave narrative, that of Olaudah Equiano, particularly his claim to have been born in Africa, his description of his homeland, and his experience in the Middle Passage.[4] The Robin Johns' story can be verified in almost every detail, and it is vital to bring to light as many firsthand accounts of the slave trade as possible. As former slaves who returned to West Africa, their case opens a window onto the creolized trading communities along the coast and the regular movement of goods, people, and ideas around the Atlantic World. We are only beginning to appreciate the full importance of these Atlantic creoles and the communities they created for the explosion of commercial and cultural exchange that revolutionized African slave-trading regions and made them central players in the Atlantic community.

1

"A Very Bloody Transaction"

Old Calabar and the Massacre of 1767

Old Town bustled on a balmy June day as its dominant slave trader, Grandy King George, and his brothers, Amboe Robin John and Ephraim Robin Robin John, and his nephew Ancona Robin Robin John prepared to lead the grand delegation soon to visit the six English slave ships anchored in the Calabar River. Hundreds of enslaved canoe boys rushed to ready the vessels that would carry scores of notable traders and their retainers out to the tall ships. Clearly this occasion was to differ from the ceremonial visits that the individual traders from the major trading "houses" customarily paid the English captains of the slavers. A fleet of nine or ten great canoes, as long as eighty feet and carrying as many as 120 men, was the center of Old Town interest as they set off to party and parley. The most gaily decorated boat carried Grandy King George, who had to present himself in a fashion that justified the title he had recently taken for himself (he had formerly been known as Ephraim Robin John). His determination to equal the majesty of the English monarch included adopting many of the trappings of English culture; the king and his sons relieved themselves in English pewter piss pots, washed in large imported brass basins, and shaved with English razors they had imported through the English slave traders. Well aware of the king's fascination with European goods and of the ambition they betokened, English slavers had supplied him with a fine "Lucking glass six foot long and six foot wide" in "a strong woden freme" that allowed the very tall and quite stout king of Old Town to admire himself from all angles. Similar mirrors reflected his sons when they too dressed as "gentlemen" in clothes whose cut, color, and style they had specified meticulously when they ordered them from England.[1]

Grandy King George presented an imposing figure as he boarded the royal canoe—dressed in a multicolored robe reaching to his knees, a red coat trimmed in gold lace, a silk sash thrown round his shoulders, a gold-headed cane in one hand, a gold-trimmed cocked hat under his arm, and a fine ceremonial sword at his side—and then made his way to the bow, where he took his place under a grand umbrella. Brightly colored ensigns fluttered in the wind, one emblazoned with his own name written in English in large letters (for the traders were literate in English).[2] Behind him a small house stood in the center of the canoe, brightly painted yellow and red, and atop the roof were two men loudly beating drums. In the bow a small cannon pointed forward, and in front of it stood a man who shook a large bundle of reeds to symbolically ward off obstacles and dangers. On each side of the canoe sat fifteen canoe boys with paddles, and between them, lined up down the center of the vessel, stood an imposing row of attendants. On most voyages these men would have been armed with cutlasses and guns, but John Ashley Hall, an English sailor on slave ships at Old Calabar in this period, reported that "when they [the Efik traders] came on board, in the common course of trade and visits, they had very few muskets in their canoes, and they are never suffered to bring their arms into the ships."[3] As the royal canoe pulled into the river it was followed by eight or nine others, all of them ornamented in the same style, though perhaps not on quite so grand a scale, occupied by the king's sons and by the "lesser gentry" of Old Town, meaning all the town's principal slave traders. Altogether, about four hundred men sailed toward the English vessels lying peacefully in the river about three miles distant from Old Town.

The purpose of this impressive visit was an invitation from the captains of the English ships to mediate a dispute then raging between the traders at Old Town and those from its commercial rival, New Town, also known as Duke Town. European ships paid "comey" or "coomey," essentially a custom's duty based on the ship's tonnage, to the king of the town with which they planned to trade, hence the rivalry between Old Town and Duke Town for the primary location on the river.

Old Town had been established probably in the mid to late seventeenth century by the ancestors of Grandy King George on a high hill overlooking a ten-mile stretch of the Calabar River, an advantageous position to capitalize on the arrival of European slave traders in Old Calabar. That trade grew from a trickle in the seventeenth century to a veritable flood in the eighteenth, when Old Calabar became one of the principal slave-exporting regions in West Africa, an expansion that made Old Town one of the most important slave suppliers in the Bight of Biafra, greatly enriched the Robin Johns, and raised the envy of other traders in Old Calabar equally eager to share the spoils. Sometime between the late seventeenth century and the mid-eighteenth, one of those families, the Dukes, originally from Creek Town, established a new trading center farther down the Calabar River at Atakpa (also known as New Town and later as Duke Town), and a long and bitter struggle ensued between Old Town and New Town for preeminence in the slave trade. The stakes were extremely high for both parties, and by 1767 matters had come to a head. The rivalry had become so intense that each side was preventing the other from sending slave-raiding expeditions up the Calabar River to purchase or capture the hundreds of men, women, and children needed to satisfy the demands of the European captains. In addition, the captains themselves had sometimes been caught between the warring factions.[4]

When the exasperated captains offered to mediate between the rulers of Old Town and New Town, Grandy King George accepted their offer to come on board the English ships for a night of festivities, then to meet on board the rulers of New Town on the following day. The king may have been a bit flattered that it was he and his entourage who had been invited as overnight guests to enjoy the hospitality that the captains offered visiting dignitaries while the New Town men would not arrive until the next day. But Grandy King George was eager to settle a dispute that impoverished both towns, and as a sign of his magnanimity and sincerity he presented one of his favorite women to Duke Ephraim, the ruler of New Town, as a wife.[5]

Duke Ephraim, Grandy King George's chief rival, was also busy making preparations for the important event to take place on the following day, but rather than decking himself and his canoes out in ceremonial splendor, he prepared for battle. Duke Ephraim was finally ready to destroy his Old Town rivals, and with the help of the English captains, he prepared a trap for the Old Town delegation. Ever since his ancestors had founded New Town generations earlier, their aim had been to supplant

Old Town and take control of the vital and profitable slave trade. Until now, however, none of his predecessors had been able to defeat the wealthy and powerful Robin Johns. Duke Ephraim had worked diligently to build alliances that would enable him to crush his opponents with remarkable speed. New Town was settled as an offshoot of an older town called Creek Town, and the rulers of New Town had maintained alliances at Creek Town whose rulers also bristled at the wealth and power of Old Town. Creek Town had long been in decline, but its fortunes revived under the leadership of Eyo Nsa (called Eyo Honesty I or Willy Honesty by the Europeans because of his honorable dealings in trade), one of the most famous and successful of the Old Calabar traders. Unlike his contemporaries in the slave trade, he was not of noble birth, and may even have been born a slave, but through marriage, hard work, intelligence, courage, and ruthlessness, he rose to the chief position in Creek Town. Eyo Honesty was as eager as Duke Ephraim to destroy the preeminence of Old Town, and the two entered into an alliance against the Robin Johns. A successful warrior, Eyo Nsa was celebrated for his bravery and feared for his cruelty. The historian David Northrup aptly describes traders like Eyo Nsa and Duke Ephraim as "men of tremendous imagination, energy, and determination who succeeded where lesser men would have failed." Although we will probably never know who laid the clever plans that defeated the Robin Johns, the scheme certainly looks like Eyo Nsa's handiwork. On the fatal morning, Eyo Nsa and Duke Ephraim readied their war canoes and hid them behind a heavily wooded turn in the river, eagerly awaiting a signal from the English ships to launch their ambush.[6]

Why should English captains intervene in Old Calabar's internal affairs? As relations between Old Town and New Town deteriorated, the English traders suffered the consequences. The English captains could either have their ships lie at anchor for months on end, with supplies running lower and lower, tempers rising higher and higher, while the traders at Old Town and New Town quarreled among themselves, or they could look for ways to force the rival traders to resume commerce. The growing rivalry between the towns threatened the peaceful conduct of trade and brought into prominence the ambiguities embedded in a commercial system based on trust and personal relationships, somewhat brittle relations that could be used both to build confidence and to deceive.

Captain James Berry of Liverpool, who had made many trading voyages to Old Calabar, expressed his outrage at the harsh treatment he received from the Robin Johns at Old Town in 1763. After anchoring his ship in the river off Old Town, he "according to custom went ashore to shake the Kings and the rest of the getlemen Hands." The Robin Johns refused to meet his terms, so

Berry forced them to trade by simply waiting on his ship for fifteen days until he wore them down to his price. But the Old Town traders were far from happy with the transaction, and Ephraim Robin John refused to give Berry his son for a pledge, as was customary. A few days later, "that rouge Ephm. [Ephraim] Robin John Joined by Rn [Robin] John Tom Robin, Captn. John Ambo and the Rest of that Town" sent out a fleet of ten war canoes to capture Berry, whom they held hostage for twenty-nine days. He reported that in order to gain his release, Grandy King George "obliged me to pay him and the Rest of the Schoundrells just what he pleas'd[;] the amount of his imposition is 4251 Copper [copper bars were the currency in Old Calabar. By contrast, Berry had paid only 1,000 coppers to the other traders for comey]." Along with the coppers, the king also took "one of my great guns . . . three of my musquetts two Blunderbusses 2 pistols [and] 2 cutlasses," arms that the king may have planned to use against his New Town rivals. To add insult to injury, the king even forced Berry "to give severall Books and one [account book] to clear him of all palaver with me." Once freed, Berry sailed downriver to trade with the Dukes at New Town, who, he reported, "I believe did me justice in every thing." Outraged by "the vilanious [*sic*] intentions of the Old Town Scoundrells," he vowed that he "never will forgive the injury Ephm and the rest of them did me till I have satisfaction."[7]

In 1764 Captain James Briggs had a violent confrontation with the Robin Johns. Though the details of their dispute do not survive, no doubt it was similar to that between the Robin Johns and Captain Berry. As the supplies of slaves dwindled and as the rivals at Old Town and New Town tried to prevent each other from acquiring and selling slaves, the English captains tried every means to force them to trade. One tactic was called rowing guard. English captains put boats into the river to stop Efik canoes. They captured the traders, and then held them hostage until they agreed to sell slaves at a reasonable price. They could also cut the Efik off from their supply of slaves by barring their passage upriver. Briggs had his chief mate lying in wait to ambush Orrock Robin John as he came down a creek in a canoe. The English sailors chased Orrock, who jumped ashore and made for the bush. When the Englishmen tried to follow, he leveled his musket and shot the first mate through the head.[8] Clearly the traders at Old Town had violated every rule that governed the trade, and their actions soon lost them the trust that was essential to maintaining successful relations.

In 1767 another English merchant at Old Calabar wrote, "There are now seven large vessels in the river, each of which expects to purchase 500 slaves, and I imagine there was seldom ever known a greater scarcity of slaves than at present." The reason for that scarcity was the ongoing struggle between Old Town and New

Town, which had grown so serious that "for a considerable time no canoe could leave their towns to go up the river for Slaves." The captain reported that "the natives are at variance with each other, and, in my opinion, it will never be ended before the destruction of all the people at Old Town, who have taken the lives of many a fine fellow . . . I now flatter myself, I shall be an assistant in revenging the just cause of every poor Englishman that have innocently suffered by them." Thanks to the reports of captains like Berry and the others, word of the arrogance and duplicity of the Old Town traders spread quickly among the small circle of slave traders in Liverpool and Bristol.[9]

In June 1767 seven English vessels lay in the river at Old Calabar: the *Indian Queen*, John Lewis, captain; the *Duke of York*, James Bivins, captain; the *Nancy*, James Maxwell, captain; the *Concord*, William Bishop, captain—all of Bristol—the *Hector*, John Washington, captain; the *Edgar*, Ambrose Lace, captain—both of Liverpool—and the *Canterbury* of London, Nonus Parke, captain. All of these captains were seasoned veterans of the trade to Old Calabar, and were well aware of the festering dispute between Old Town and New Town. European traders usually ignored internal disputes among the traders at Old Calabar, but given the disastrous impact of the dispute on the supply of slaves, combined with the actions of the Old Town traders, the captains clearly favored the traders at New Town. Whether the English captains, Eyo Nsa, or Duke Ephraim actually devised the plot to destroy the Robin Johns is unclear, but they all found themselves with that goal in mind.[10]

Without the connivance of the English captains, the plot could not have succeeded. Most of the captains agreed that it was time to punish the Robin Johns for their effrontery and reopen the trade. Captains Bivins, Lace, Lewis, Maxwell, and Parke addressed several letters to the Robin Johns and the Old Town men inviting them to meet the traders from New Town aboard their ships, where the captains would serve as mediators to settle the dispute. The captains gave the Robin Johns assurances that they would be protected on their ships, probably the only conceivable place in Old Calabar where such assurances could have been given and the only neutral ground where each side could feel secure. Further, since the Efik were not permitted to carry arms on board the English ships and had few weapons in their canoes, if attacked, the Old Town men would be "incapable of resisting."[11]

After spending a pleasant night on board the English ships, no doubt fed well and plied with drink in keeping with the usual tenor of such visits, the men from Old Town awoke early to begin preparations for their important meeting. Grandy King George, his son Otto Ephraim, his younger brothers, Amboe and Little Ephraim Robin John, and his nephew Ancona Robin Robin John spent the night on board the *Indian Queen*. On the following morning, Captain Lewis asked Amboe, Little Ephraim, and Ancona to deliver a letter to Captain Lace. Meanwhile, the canoes were busy carrying men to the other ships. From the *Edgar*, Amboe, Little Ephraim, and Ancona took letters to Captains Maxwell, Parke, and Bivins. When the Robin Johns boarded the *Duke of York*, Bivins, apparently acting on a signal from Lace, ordered armed men to trap the brothers in the cabin while other men opened fire on the canoes alongside the ship. The Robin Johns were relaxing in the cabin when Captain Bivins and his first mate came in with pistols drawn. Amboe rushed the men and knocked them both to the floor, but more crewmen quickly followed, well armed with cutlasses. Ancona later recalled that the sailors "were Cutting him on ye head and he cryed out, O Capt. Bevan, what fashion is this, for white men to kill black men fo [for]?"[12] Little Ephraim and Ancona tried to make their escape through the cabin window, but sailors knocked them down and locked them in irons.

Meanwhile Captain Lewis ordered his chief mate, William Floyd, to watch for a jack to fly from the mizzenmast of the *Hector*, the signal for the attack on the Old Town delegation to begin. As Floyd watched for the signal, he was surprised to hear small arms fire coming from the *Duke of York*. As Floyd looked on, he saw sailors firing into a canoe alongside the ship; it quickly filled with water as the men on board tried to swim to safety. Once the *Duke of York* initiated the attack, three of the other English ships opened fire (the *Hector* and the *Concord* did not; their captains apparently refused to join the ambush) while the war canoes from New Town and Creek Town emerged from their concealed positions and joined in the massacre. The English captains ordered their men into small boats, where they joined in the slaughter of the Old Town men swimming in the river. The river literally ran red with blood.[13]

The captives were transported to the English ships as the massacre came to its bloody conclusion. Eyo Nsa and a group of men from New Town pulled their war canoe up alongside the *Duke of York*. Bivins consulted with Captain Parke and ordered his first mate, Mr. Green, to deliver Amboe to the people of New Town. Green refused, but Eyo Nsa said, "By god, captain Parke, if you give me that man to cutty head, I'll give you the best man in my canoe . . . and you shall be slaved the first ship." That promise was enough for Bivins, who ignored Amboe's desperate pleas and ordered the transfer once Eyo Nsa handed over a man from his canoe. Amboe begged for a drink of water, but even that was denied him as he was lowered into the canoe. Eyo Nsa grabbed him by his hair, held him over the gunwale of the boat, and beheaded him with one blow as Little Ephraim and Ancona looked on in horror. Eyo Nsa waved the bloody head in the air as shouts of victory rose from the New Town and Creek Town canoes. Eyo Nsa wanted Captain Bivins to turn over Little Ephraim and Ancona as well, but Bivins kept them on board his ship, promising to turn them over once his ship was slaved as agreed.[14]

Grandy King George, on board the *Edgar*, barely escaped with his life. Captain Lace recalled that he and the king were about to have breakfast at eight o'clock that morning. Lace was pouring a cup of coffee when he heard firing. Lace reported that the frightened king jumped overboard while ordering his son and nephew to stay behind. But one English sailor told a different story. When crewmen on the *Edgar* attempted to capture Grandy King George, he fought bravely and killed two of his English attackers. He jumped overboard and climbed into a little canoe known as a one-man canoe, and paddled desperately toward the shore. One of the English ships fired a six-pounder at the canoe, and one well-aimed shot struck the small craft and shattered it to pieces. The king survived, however, and managed to swim to shore. Despite eleven wounds from musket shot, he escaped to Old Town, with his enemies at his heels. A surgeon from one of the English ships that had not joined in the attack treated the king and helped save his life.[15]

Fortunately for Little Ephraim and Ancona, Captain Bivins was not a man of his word. Even after his ship was slaved, he refused to deliver his two captives and instead sailed away with them. The two princes of Old Calabar joined other survivors of the massacre and slaves supplied by New Town in the stinking holds below the decks of the *Duke of York*, en route to the Caribbean with its valuable cargo. Their capture provoked a flurry of desperate letters from their family in Old Town to English slave traders. Orrock Robin John wrote to Thomas Jones, one of the veterans of the trade with long-standing connections in Old Town, asking for the return of "Lettle Ephraim & Ancone." He also assured Jones that his family was eager to reenter the slave trade and that they held no grudges toward the captains who had participated in the massacre, and pleaded with Jones to boycott New Town. Grandy King George himself wrote Jones at about the same time, also asking for the return of his relatives and for a resumption of the trade. Lace took the king's son, Otto Ephraim, back to England with him. Lace later wrote, "I brought young Epm. home, and had him at School near two years, then sent him out, he cost me above sixty pounds and when his Fathers gone I hope the son will be a good man."[16] While Otto Ephraim was safe in England, the whereabouts of Little Ephraim and Ancona was unknown in Old Calabar. Despite their relatives' desperate pleas, it would be many years before anyone in Old Calabar had news of their fate.

The Massacre of 1767 completely altered the politics of Old Calabar. Some four hundred men from Old Town were slaughtered, a loss that devastated Grandy King George's trading house and left his world in shambles. On a personal level, the king had lost his brothers,

Amboe and Little Ephraim, his son Otto Ephraim, and his nephew Ancona. Despite the fact that Grandy King George survived, his crushing defeat and the deaths of so many of the gentlemen traders and valuable canoe boys led to the virtual collapse of Old Town. When Captain George Colley of the *Latham* visited Old Calabar on a slave-trading expedition in 1768, he reported that "our purchase here [Old Town] at present is very small, owing to a hot and troublesome war among the natives." Problems with English merchants continued as well. In 1773 the *Integrity* of Liverpool (Richard Jackson, captain) and the *Maria* of Bristol (George Bishop, captain) arrived at Old Town to trade. After a dispute over the comey payments, Jackson fired on Old Town for twenty-four hours until the king's bribes stopped the assault. Jackson warned the king that if he "went on bord of Bishop I shuld be stopped by him and my hed cut of and sent to the Duke at Nuetown." In addition, the king charged that Jackson had sailed away with his pawns after he had taken on his full cargo of slaves, a loss that included four of the king's sons. Captain Jackson, well aware of the king's weakened position and the rivalry with New Town, could manipulate the king in ways unthinkable before the massacre. In 1773, the king pleaded with Captain Lace to "send good ship and make me grandy again for war take two much copr [copper] from me."[17] Despite Grandy King George's attempts to rebuild his house, Old Town never recovered from the massacre and fell further and further behind its New Town rival.

This is the version of events that best fits the evidence. But in 1790 the British House of Commons conducted hearings on the African slave trade and investigated the events that took place in the Calabar River in 1767, and in those hearings testimony from one English slaver gave a different version of events. The committee called Ambrose Lace, captain of the *Edgar* of Liverpool during the massacre, and one of the most important slave traders in Liverpool. By 1790 he had spent about forty years in the trade, first as a crewman, then as a captain, and finally as the owner of slave ships. As a captain, he transported over 2,700 Africans to the slave colonies in the Americas. During those voyages over 450 captives died, and were unceremoniously tossed overboard to be eaten by the sharks that trailed the vessels of death. As an owner, he invested in the transport of over 15,400 men, women, and children, of whom only about 12,600 arrived in the New World. When he entered the business in the 1740s, it was an accepted area of commerce with few opponents, but Lace lived to see a dramatic shift in public opinion about the trade, symbolized by the parliamentary hearing of 1790, which was a direct outgrowth of public petitions against slave trading. The historian David Brion Davis referred to this change as a "remarkable shift in moral consciousness," characterized by the growing belief that the slave trade and New World slavery "symbolized all the forces that threatened the true destiny of man."[18] No doubt Lace pondered the changed climate as he recalled the events of 1767. He made his way through the bustling streets of London to the House of Parliament, where he answered the summons of the Select Committee. The hardened old captain took his seat as questioning began:

Was you ever employed in the African Trade?
Yes.
Was you at Old Calabar in the year 1767, as captain of any, and of what ship?
I was there as captain in the ship Edgar.
What number of ships were then lying at Calabar?
Nine.
Were they all ships concerned in the African Trade?
Every one.
Do you remember, that in order to make an end of a dispute which had for some time subsisted between the inhabitants of the Old and New Town, any agreement was made for both parties to meet on shipboard?
Yes.
Can you describe the nature of that dispute?
There had been for many years a dispute between the people of Old Town and New Town.
State the nature and circumstances of that dispute.

*When I first went there in 1748, there were no inhabitants
in the place called Old Town, they all lived at the place
called New Town; some time after disputes arose between
a party who now call themselves Old Town people, and
those who are now called New Town people.*

When the parties were invited to meet on ship-board,
was that invitation made with an insidious view, to
get them within the power of the English, to make
Slaves of them?

No.

Did any of the parties meet on board in consequence of
such agreement; and what passed on that occasion?

*The principal people from Old Town came on board my
ship, where the duke (the principal man of Old Town)
was to have met them; they came on board about half
past seven in the morning; at about eight I was going to
breakfast with a person who called himself king of Old
Town; there were four of the king's large canoes alongside of my ship, where the other canoes were I cannot
tell: I was just pouring out some coffee, when I heard a
firing. I went upon deck along with the king, and my
people told me my gunner was killed; immediately the
king was for going overboard; I then told him to stay
where he was; he told me he would not, he would go in
his canoe, which he did; the firing, by what I can recol-
lect, might be for ten or fifteen minutes, but I cannot be
certain as to the exact time. The canoes . . . most of
them then got astern of my ship within about 300 or 400*

yards; I had not time to make observations of the two
parties, I wanted to defend myself after I was fired into;
I was no further molested, the canoes were all gone.

At the time the firing commenced, were any of your
guns loaded, or were any of the small arms in the
possession of your crew?

*The small arms are always loaden, but they were locked
up, and the chest was broke open.*

Was the key of the chest afterwards found, and where?

In the gunner's pocket.

Did you or your people take any share in the affray that
then happened?

No more than any gentleman in this room.

Were any guns fired from your ship, great or small,
upon that occasion?

No; not so much as a pistol.

Were any guns fired from any other ships upon that occasion?

Not to my knowledge.

Did the king kill any man on board your ship?

No.

Was the king on board any other ship during the battle?

*Not to my knowledge; if he was, it must have been before
he came on board my ship.*

Were there any Slaves actually made on that occasion?

Not to my knowledge.

At what time, and how long after, did you get the com-
plement of Slaves for your ship?

I went there in the beginning of July, I cannot exactly state when this happened, and sailed the first week of December; I was there within a few days of five months, over or under.

Did the English enter into this business with any fraudulent or improper view?

Not that I ever heard of.

Did the English, as you know or believe, reap any benefit whatever from this transaction?

No; it was against the trade.

Previous to this transaction, had there been any consultation amongst the English captains, relative to the difference between the Old and New Towns, or relative to any other matter connected with this transaction?

If there was, it was before I came into the river, and unknown to me.[19]

Was Captain Lace telling the truth? Were he and the other English captains innocent in the Massacre of 1767? There is little evidence to support his version of events. Lace showed a very poor understanding of the history of Old Calabar (suggesting that Old Town came into existence *after* New Town, for instance), and appeared to have no real knowledge of the dispute between Old Town and New Town. A letter he wrote to Thomas Jones in 1773 revealed a very different understanding of

Old Calabar. He carefully recited the genealogy of the Robin John family and reported that "as to Grandy Epm. [Grandy King George or Duke Ephraim] you know very well [he] has been Guilty of many bad Act[i]ons, no man can say anything in his favor, a History of his life would exceed any of our Pirates, the whole sett at Old Town you know as well as me." Lace took one of Grandy King George's sons back to England with him after the massacre, sent him to school, and returned him to Old Calabar almost two years later.[20] It is inconceivable that Lace's memory could have been as faulty as it appeared in his testimony.

It comes as no surprise that Lace did his best to defend his actions and those of the other English captains. The Massacre of 1767 was the most egregious case of English slavers' use of violence to interfere in the internal politics of Old Calabar. They did so, of course, with the expectation that their activities would never come to light. Their actions clearly violated the Acts of Parliament for Regulating the Slave Trade, which stipulated that "no commander or master of any ship trading to Africa shall by fraud, force or violence or by any indirect practice whatsoever take on board or carry away from the coast of Africa any negro or native of the said country or commit or suffer to be committed any violence to the natives to the prejudice of the said trade." And now Lace found himself, and the entire trade, on trial in the court of public opinion. He must have cursed his luck that the episode had ever come to light and that it continued to be a subject of investigation nearly twenty years later.[21]

Grandy King George humiliated, defeated; Amboe Robin John, dead; Little Ephraim Robin Robin John and Ancona Robin Robin John, princes of Old Town and slavers themselves, now enslaved. Four hundred of the gentry and canoe boys of Old Town massacred or enslaved. Duke Ephraim and Eyo Nsa triumphant. The English captains, their slave ships now loaded and the troublesome Robin Johns of Old Town brought low, sail away with their ships loaded with slaves and fully satisfied with the outcome of events. It certainly was, as one of the English captains described it in the language of commerce, "a very bloody transaction."[22]

These are the chief protagonists of the Massacre of 1767, but if we are to fully understand how this event came to pass, why the traders of Old Calabar willingly slaughtered one another, and why English ship captains actively plotted an attack against men they routinely referred to as friends and gentlemen, we must delve into the history of Old Calabar. And if we are to fully grasp the long-range implications of the massacre, we must carry the story forward, especially the story of Little Ephraim and Ancona, whose capture and enslavement sent them on a remarkable journey around the Atlantic World.

2

"Nothing But Sivellety and Fare Trade"

Old Calabar and the Impact of the Slave Trade on an African Society

In 1773 Grandy King George urged English slave traders to come to Old Calabar with promises of "Nothing but Sivellety [Civility] and fare [fair] trade."[1] That the king was able to write to English merchants in English, and that his promise of favorable trade was couched in the language of civility prevalent in the eighteenth century, says a great deal about the evolution of the slave trade in this distinctive region. Several characteristics of Old Calabar's history and development paved the way for it to become a major slave-trading society. The Efik, a branch of the Ibibio-speaking people, were traders with well-developed long-distance networks stretching from one of the best harbors on the west coast of Africa deep into the interior, networks that could easily be turned toward the slave trade when that opportunity presented itself. Their semiautonomous towns, dominated by well-structured, kinship-based merchant houses, provided ideal institutions to facilitate the trade and gave them the necessary political and military strength to control it and to ensure that Europeans did not gain a foothold in their territory. The Efik were also remarkably adaptable. The introduction of the trade demanded major changes in their social, economic, and cultural life, changes that the Efik made quickly as the slave trade grew to dominate their economy.[2]

Old Calabar, part of the Lower Guinea coast in present-day Nigeria, lies in the curve of the African shoreline just where the Bight of Biafra is separated from the Bight of Benin by the Niger River delta.[3] The Cross River provided one of the best harbors in West Africa, and the larger Cross River network provided the Efik with access far into the interior. At its mouth the river stretches ten or twelve miles across and remains that wide up to Parrot Island, about thirty miles from the coast. Above that island, the Cross River meets the Calabar, and small, marshy islands crowd the river. Below Parrot Island, the river banks were low and marshy, covered with mangrove swamps. "Efik" is derived from the Ibibio verb *fik,* which means "to oppress," a name given to them by other Ibibio-speaking people who came into conflict with them. The Efik adopted the name despite its negative connotations, but also referred to themselves as Iboku, derived from two Ibo words meaning those who quarrel with the Ibo. Both names suggest that the relations between the Efik and their neighbors were once hostile, and according to one legend, the Efik settlements originated from that hostility, but by the seventeenth century, when the first Europeans arrived, the Efik were carrying on a thriving trade with the Ibo and others.[4]

Whatever the motivation for their emigration, evidence suggests that by the early to mid sixteenth century the Efik had established their settlements in the Cross River estuary, where they lived primarily as fishermen and traders. They carried on an active commerce, exchanging coastal products, particularly fish and salt, for agricultural products, especially yams and palm oil, from Ibo people in the interior. The principal Efik towns were built up the Calabar River, about thirty miles from the coast, where the mangrove swamps gave way to higher ground. Their first major settlement, called Ikot Etundo (Creek Town by Europeans), was situated on a creek connecting the Cross and Calabar rivers. When the English trader John Barbot visited Old Calabar in the late seventeenth century, he found the area to be "well furnish'd with villages and hamlets all about, where Europeans drive their trade with the Blacks, who are good civiliz'd people." The fact that Barbot regarded the Efik as civilized suggests that good relations between them and the Europeans were already well established, and Barbot reported that Old Calabar was a principal trading post for English slavers. He noted payments to to several traders, including "duke Aphrom" (Ephraim) and "king Robin," the ancestors of Duke Ephraim and Grandy King George. Barbot's account suggests that Old Town and New Town were already in existence when he arrived there. Efik towns ranged in population from 1,000 to 5,000 people, and were divided into sections or wards. The members of a ward considered themselves to be descendants of their ward's founder, and might be further divided into the descendants of a son or grandson of the founder. These lineages were known as houses. Each ward had a head and a council of elders, but before the rise of the slave trade there was no centralized authority. The European title of "king" appears in early slave trader accounts from the late seventeenth century, but the title was an honorific one adopted by the leading Efik traders who were heads of a local community or an important ward (called *obong* by the Efik) and did not imply the existence of a monarchy based on the European model. The head of a ward or other subdivision of a town was called a duke, a title that some elite traders considered "higher and more expressive of power than that of King." Creek Town consisted of three houses: Eyo Ema, Atai Ema, and Effiom Ekpo. Creek Town grew and prospered until conflict between the Eyo Ema and Atai Ema houses resulted in the establishment of

Obutong (Old Town) by members of Atai Ema, the ancestors of the Robin Johns. The exact date of this division is unknown, but Old Town certainly existed by the late seventeenth century, when it appears in European records.[5]

Slavery was well established among the Efik before the rise of the European slave trade, as it was across most of West Africa, but slavery may have played a more important economic role among the Efik than among other coastal groups. Nearby coastal states like Bonny and Elem Kalabari were located in mangrove swamps and had to import much of their food; they had little need for large numbers of enslaved laborers. The situation was different in Old Calabar, which had a fertile hinterland that could be profitably farmed with enslaved labor, and the Efik had a market for their products with their trading partners in the interior. Barbot found that slaves were essentially "a form of money among these Africans." He observed that individuals were enslaved through a variety of means: "Slaves are either those who, having no means of subsistence, sell themselves to rich men for life, or those taken in war, or children sold by their parents because they cannot keep them, or finally, those sold as slaves because they cannot pay the fines to which they have been condemned. But of all these, the largest number are those taken in war or seized in their homes and carried off." Initially, slaves were drawn from among the Efik themselves, and the system was not based on ethnic or racial differences. Slaves referred to their owners as "father" and "mother." As one of the slave traders reported in 1773, "You know very well the custom of that place whatever Man or Woman gos to live in any family they take the Name of the first man in the family and call him Father." The missionary Hope Waddell, who resided in Old Calabar in the mid-nineteenth century, recorded the various ways that people could fall into slavery. Although it is problematic to read backward from such sources, the means of enslavement that he described were consistent with the practices that Barbot observed and with those followed in other parts of Africa in the eighteenth century. According to Waddell, slaves came from several sources, and scholars of African slavery agree that "there were numerous ways to enslave people." In Old Calabar, as in other regions, individuals sold themselves into slavery to escape famine, to seek protection, or to improve their circumstances, since a well-placed slave might prosper more than an impoverished free man. Individuals could also be enslaved for debts, and entire families could fall into slavery by that means. James Morley, a sailor on board slave ships at Old Calabar in the 1770s, reported that he knew of persons who were sold because they committed adultery or theft. Among those sold for adultery was one of the wives of Duke Ephraim, though the woman, who spoke very good English, told Morley that she was innocent of the crime, and since Ephraim treated her "with the greatest civility" when he brought her on board, Morley believed the charge to be false. Men might also be enslaved as punishment for crimes or taken as prisoners of war, but those enslaved in these ways were generally in a worse position than other slaves; their lives were considered forfeit and they might be subject to sacrifice or sale, unlike those enslaved by other means. In Waddell's day, a common maxim in Old Calabar was that a person could easily fall into slavery, but could seldom recover his freedom. Slaves could not purchase their freedom, and indeed if a master freed a slave the act often was seen as a disgrace to the slave, who had to find another master to protect him or suffer the worst possible abuses. Slaves could, however, improve their position by acquiring slaves of their own, which would free them from hard labor and raise their status. If an enslaved concubine bore her master's children, both she and the children became free.[6]

Old Calabar accounted for the export of over 17,000 slaves from 1725 to 1750, and the trade increased dramatically from 1750 to 1775, when the number of persons exported soared to over 62,000. All told, approximately 1.2 million slaves were transported from the Cross and Niger Rivers in the eighteenth century. Merchants in Bristol and Liverpool dominated the trade from Old Calabar, and approximately 85 percent of the slaves exported from the area left on English ships.[7]

On the African side, the trade was controlled by Old

Calabar merchants like the Robin Johns who used the profits from the trade and the firearms they acquired to expand their power in the region. Because of their increasing wealth, Efik communities grew in size and number in the seventeenth and eighteenth centuries as the slave trade expanded, and this growth accounted for the subdivisions of lineage groups and other changes within their society. Successful slave traders required more and more canoes, manned by more and more slaves, and became the masters of large numbers of dependents. Before the expansion of the slave trade, the oldest member of the family was head of the house, but as the trade grew leadership passed to the wealthiest member of the house (called Etubom, father of the canoe, as opposed to Ete Ufok, father of the house). David Northrup has outlined the three major features of canoe houses that set them apart from the old lineage houses: first, the canoe houses expanded rapidly with the growth of the slave trade and the addition of slaves from the interior; second, the leaders of the canoe houses were "men of talent promoted rigorously from among slave and free members alike who demonstrated the necessary abilities"; and third, canoe houses "formed a single economic unit, a sort of trading company." The new title Etubom highlights the importance canoes played in the lives of the traders who could launch large fleets of them. The change retained the patriarchal structure of Efik society, but downplayed the importance of lineage as larger numbers of persons who were not truly related were incorporated into the houses. These increasingly large and powerful trading houses commanded the labor of hundreds or even thousands of enslaved rowers, soldiers, relatives, domestics, agricultural workers, and other dependents, and wealth was measured by the number of people the Etubom commanded. The Etubom used European trade goods not only to acquire slaves for sale to Europeans, but also to attract followers, since goods were also distributed among dependents. Houses used slave labor to farm plantations, where they raised crops for consumption as well as to supply the slave ships. Along with the male slaves came their families and the extended infrastructure necessary to support them. Houses that grew rich enough and large enough were essentially able to establish themselves as new lineage groups, though they still acknowledged their descent from the original lineage founders. Originally, the Efik were divided into two lineage groups, but as the slave trade expanded, the two subdivided into seven wards or city-states. Given their skills as traders, their trade networks to the interior, and their fleets of canoes capable of ferrying large numbers of people, the Efik were well positioned to capitalize on the arrival of European merchants.[8]

Europeans had no onshore base or factory in Old Calabar as they did in some parts of West Africa, and the Efik refused to allow them to permanently reside there. When ships arrived, they stopped inside the river's mouth at Parrot Island and fired a cannon to signal their arrival. A response was fired from shore, and a native pilot was sent to lead the ship upriver. European ships paid comey to the king of the town with which they planned to trade, hence the rivalry between Old Town and New Town for the primary location on the river. Once the comey was paid, Old Calabar kings and chiefs, referred to as the "gentlemen of the towns," kept up a lively social intercourse with the Europeans, known as the "gentlemen of the river." The Ekif entertained Europeans on the shore, and the Europeans returned the hospitality on board their ships. Such festivities were essential before trade negotiations could begin. English captains soon learned the best times to arrive in Old Calabar to trade. Barbot reported that it was best for European traders to arrive in Old Calabar from May to September. Yams could not be harvested before July, so after that date provisions could be purchased more cheaply. May and June were also advantageous because continual rains kept the heat down and allowed the Efik to devote their full attention to acquiring slaves from the interior, "and are consequently the fittest time for us to purchase slaves with expedition, and less hindrance and fatigue." October, November, and December were considered the worst months for trade because of the dry, scorching heat and the harmattan winds that blew in from the deserts to the north and created a haze so dense "that it is not possible to see from one end of the ship to the other." English ships might remain at anchor for months or as long as a year before they acquired their full cargo of slaves. During that time, the Europeans lived on their ships, roofing them with palm thatch for some relief from the tropical sun. Sailors were not idle; they unloaded the cargoes of trade goods so that the ship's carpenters could build the platforms in which the slaves would travel across the Atlantic. As the trade goods and supplies were unloaded from the holds, the ship's carpenters transformed the lower deck by building the platforms along the sides of the ship, so close that each captive had only a few feet of space. John Newton reported that "their lodging-rooms below the deck, which are three (for the men, the boys, and the women), besides a place for the sick, are sometimes more than five feet high, and sometimes less; and this height is divided towards the middle, for the slaves lie in two rows, one above the other, on each side of the ship, close to each other, like books upon a shelf."[9]

English traders and the Old Calabar elite communicated with one another in English or in a "trade language" consisting predominantly of English words but using an African grammatical structure, and elite members of the trading houses like Little Ephraim and Ancona were fluent in both the spoken and written versions of the trade language. Theirs is one of several West African trade languages that emerged from Gambia to Cameroon which the linguist Ian Hancock refers to as "English-based Atlantic Creoles." Not simply a pidgin English, this creolized language was a hybrid combining linguistic influences from various sources into a new and fully complete language with its own systemic structure, and it even became a mother tongue. The evolution of such languages and their adoption all along the West African coast and their transfer to the Americas illustrates the complexities of cross-cultural contact and the ongoing transformations that the slave trade brought about.[10]

One English sailor who visited Old Calabar reported that "all of them [the African traders] speak English, some of them very good," and another agreed that "the Black Traders of . . . Calabar . . . are very expert at reckoning and talking the different Languages of their own Country and those of the Europeans." Many of the leading merchants of Old Calabar were also literate in English and creole; they kept their own accounts, sometimes inspected English slave traders' account books, corresponded directly with English merchants, and some even kept diaries. Surviving letters between English and Efik traders show that close personal relationships developed between them, relationships reinforced by regular correspondence that included expressions of endearment and even small gifts to traders' wives and children. That ability to communicate directly was especially important in a commercial system based on face-to-face negotiation and an understanding of character. Efik merchants and their English counterparts understood the prevailing convention that "letters of trade, wrote with judgement, and language suitable to the subject, beget respect and confidence." Although it is not clear how Little Ephraim and Ancona mastered the trade language, in some cases, the African traders arranged to send their sons to England for further education, often at the encouragement of the English traders. As a group of Liverpool traders reported, "It has always been the Practice of Merchants and Commanders of Ships trading to Africa, to encourage the Natives to send their Children to England, as it not only conciliates their Friendship and softens their Manners, but adds greatly to the Security of the Trader, which answers the Purposes both of Interest and Humanity." An English education also had benefits for the African traders; as one of the Liverpool traders noted, "The motives which principally induce the Natives of Africa . . . to send their Children to England, are to receive such an Education as will fit them for trading with greater Advantage, as the Trade is principally carried on by trusting the Goods to different Hands, and sometimes to a very large Amount. The Acquisition of that Knowledge gives them a confessed Superiority over their less informed Countrymen, which by associating with the Whites and following their Manners, they are ever after studious to retain." He observed that "the Prevalence of Example have diffused among the Natives a Love of Society and a Desire for the Ornaments of Dress and Conveniences of Life."[11]

The English traders noted that the Old Calabar slave

traders sent their sons to England to learn English manners and to create the personal bonds vital to the trade. The quest for civility on the part of the African merchants does not reflect some European cultural project aimed at overcoming African savagery or remaking natives in their own image. Rather, African merchant elites sought to adopt the trappings of civility in order to bridge the distinctions that separated them from their European trading partners, a venture that the English slavers encouraged. Young men like Little Ephraim and Ancona were carefully groomed to play essential roles in trade with English merchants, developing skills that served them well later. The quest for civility functioned also as a marker within Old Calabar's society. Elite slave traders carried many aspects of their quest for civility into their internal relations so that European dress, language, dining utensils, and other luxury goods linked them together as members of a self-fashioned elite. Most important, the traders of Old Calabar used their knowledge of the English language, their ability to keep in touch with favored English merchants through correspondence, and a conscious adoption of English customs and conventions to facilitate trade. For instance, when Antera Duke and his companions went to dinner on a slave ship, he recorded that "we three dressed as white men." Similarly, when he entertained Englishmen on shore, he wrote, "we wore fine hats and fine clothes and handkerchiefs. All the Captains and we gentlemen had dinner." Traders in Old Calabar followed many of the conventions that governed polite communication in the eighteenth century. They often closed their letters to England with greetings to traders' wives and other family members and sometimes sent them gifts of ivory or other exotic goods. This was part of an effort to create lasting commercial relationships based in part on feelings. Indeed, the letters between the African and English slave traders bear many of the marks of courtship epistles. For instance, in 1761 the Liverpool trader William Earle assured his Old Calabar counterpart Duke Abashy that "You know very well I love all Calabar, I do not want to wrong." Old Calabar traders tried to woo the English merchants to trade with promises of rewards. As Grandy King George wrote his "friend" Thomas Jones of Bristol, "I hop you send ships for My oun Water. I will slaves you ship & Desire all Marchant in Bristol to them."[12] Little Ephraim and Ancona, like most young elite members of a prominent canoe house, had mastered these epistolary conventions.

If traders happened to be in Old Calabar on Christmas or New Year's Eve, Efik gentlemen arranged parties to celebrate the occasions. Among the items of trade Old Calabar merchants requested were fashionable clothes, dinner ware and eating utensils, furniture, ink and paper; and some prominent traders in Old Calabar used joiners and carpenters from slave ships to help build their houses in the English style. The trappings of English culture helped confirm Old Calabar traders' status as gentlemen worthy of trust in financial dealings. English traders advanced credit in the form of trade goods, which could amount to substantial sums, a practice referred to as "trust." As Liverpool slave traders noted, "the Trade [at Old Calabar] is principally carried on by trusting the Goods to different Hands, and sometimes to a very large Amount." The English ships carried out large cargoes of trade goods, including fabrics, brass and copper kettles and pans, pewter basins, iron pots, bars of iron and lead, plates, dishes, wineglasses, knives, spoons, razors, soap, gunpowder and muskets, rum and brandy, beads and other trinkets, laced hats, jackets, mirrors, axes, hatchets, and cutlasses. As security, the traders turned over "pawns," often their own sons or daughters, to be held on board the slave ships until the debts were settled. Using this system was another way that members of the elite trading families came to know the English traders well and vice versa. The development of the system of credit and pawnship was essential to the expansion of the slave trade and gave the African traders access to the British capital that allowed them to become important figures in the emerging Atlantic economy. This system occasionally broke down, and letters from Old Calabar's rulers sometimes complained that their sons had been taken away by mistake. For example, in 1773 Grandy King George complained to Ambrose Lace about Captain Richard Jackson, who had carried away several pawns; the angry king wrote, "you may think Sir that it was vary vaxing to have my sons caried of by Captn Jackson and Robbin sons and the King of Qua son . . . and yet thy say I do them bad." Such events could seriously damage trade relations, and the Efik traders sometimes held all captains responsible for such acts until their pawns were returned to them. Captains were often willing to find and return lost pawns in an effort to better their own position in the trade. John Newton, for example, redeemed a free boy who had been taken away illegally to Rhode Island and returned him to his home.[13]

The Old Calabar traders did not keep slaves on hand ready for trade, but rather acquired them after a ship arrived and a deal had been struck. The traders took the goods advanced to them by the English traders, and set out upriver in their war canoes. Fleets might have as few as three or as many as a dozen canoes, each of which carried up to 120 people and measured up to eighty feet long. Led by the heads of the canoe houses, their sons, and other relatives or lieutenants, the canoes were manned by a crew of forty to fifty enslaved "canoe boys" who paddled the craft, twenty to thirty traders, and other armed men. In addition, each canoe had a three- or four-pound cannon lashed to the bow. These expeditions lasted from ten days to three weeks. Little Ephraim and Ancona were probably of an age to have participated in these raids. Using the extensive Cross River network as their highway or traveling over land, the traders sought out slaves, often from Aro merchants, members of the Igbo ethnic group, who built a successful commercial network that reached from the Niger delta up the Cross River into Ibibio and Igbo country. Skilled in the use of firearms, the Aro employed mercenary soldiers who acquired slaves, but their trade relied primarily on judicial activity and kidnapping of individuals rather than all-out war. They established trade settlements and market fairs, and contracted with local merchants for the purchase of slaves. Through the Ekif, they obtained the credit they needed to expand their operations. Even with fleets of ten canoes, it required many expeditions for the Efik to fill a slave ship, and the Cross River was often crowded with many ships from several nations, though the overwhelming majority came from England and France. Most of the slaves exported from Old Calabar throughout its involvement in the trade were drawn from people of the Igbo and Ibibio language groups who lived in a densely populated region between the Niger and Cross rivers. Their small village system left them vulnerable and made it possible for the Efik to rely on raiding as one source of slaves far longer than most suppliers along the coast were able to do. One Englishman participated in a slaving expedition from Old Calabar in 1787 made up of twelve canoes. He reported that during the day the traders "called at the villages we passed, and purchased our slaves fairly," but at night they raided villages and captured as many men, women, and children as possible. Another sailor "heard from the Traders and Canoe Boys of Bonny and Calabar, that some of the Slaves sold to the Europeans . . . have become so in consequence of Debt, and others in consequence of Crimes. The great Bulk of them, however, . . . were . . . taken in piratical Excursions, or by Treachery and Surprise." The Ekif traders probably acquired most of their slaves from the Aro, but as eighteenth-century sources suggest, they continued to launch surprise raids on villages themselves, a practice that may have increased when the usual supplies were inadequate.[14]

The Efik packed their canoes with slaves, generally twenty or thirty in each canoe. Some slaves, particularly the men, had their arms tied behind their backs with twigs and grass ropes, and a few were pinioned above the knees as well. They were thrown into the bottoms of the canoes, often in pain and nearly covered with water, until they made the journey to Old Calabar. Once the canoes landed, the slaves were taken to the traders' houses, where they were fed and their skin was oiled to make them appear healthier. The traders then summoned the Europeans to inspect them. Generally, the captain and the doctor of the English slavers examined the slaves and made their purchases. Prices were computed in copper bars. When Barbot traded in Old Calabar in the late seventeenth century, he found that male slaves cost from forty to forty-eight coppers, women from twenty-eight to thirty-six, boys from twenty to forty, and girls from seventeen to thirty. At the same time he paid sixty coppers for forty baskets of plantains. Once purchased, the slaves were transported in groups of forty to fifty, sometimes in the traders' canoes, sometimes in the ships' boats, to the ships, where they were housed belowdecks. Some of the slaves, the men in particular, were put into irons for the duration of the Middle Passage.[15]

Isaac Parker, a sailor on board an English slaver in Old Calabar, left a rare firsthand account of slave raids into the interior. Parker sailed from Liverpool in 1765 on board the *Latham*, with Captain George Colley. Colley was a harsh man who alienated many of his crewmen, including Parker, during the nine months they spent at Old Calabar. Parker's major cause of dissatisfaction was the poor rations Colley handed out to the crew. The complaint may seem trivial, but undernourishment could cause serious illnesses among sailors. Parker may well have feared that poor rations on the African coast, where supplies were plentiful, were likely to get worse during the Middle Passage, with potentially terrifying results. He was frequently on shore at the house of Dick Ebro, a "great trader" at New Town, transporting slaves from the shore to the *Latham*. When the ship had taken on its full cargo of slaves and prepared to sail for America, Parker deserted the ship and appealed to Dick Ebro for protection. The African trader locked him in one of his rooms for three days until the *Latham* set sail.[16]

Afterward, Parker lived for five months with Dick

Ebro, and spent his time fishing, hunting parrots, and cleaning the large supply of arms, pistols, and blunderbusses owned by the trader. On one occasion, Dick Ebro asked, "Parker, will you go to war with me?" Parker agreed. He watched as the canoes were fitted out with ammunition, cutlasses, pistols, powder and balls, and two three-pound cannons affixed to blocks of wood for each canoe, one for the stern, another for the bow. The party paddled up the river in the daytime, but when they approached a village, they hid under the bush along the riverbank until nightfall, when they pulled the canoes ashore. They left two or three men in each canoe, then raided the village, capturing everyone they could see, handcuffing them, and carrying them to the canoes. They did the same farther up the river, until they had captured forty-five slaves—men, women, and children. The party then returned to New Town, scattered the slaves among different houses, and sent word to the captains of the many slave ships that slaves were now available. The traders made no effort to keep families together; only nursing children remained with their mothers. The captains then sent a couple of men in boats to collect the slaves and transport them to the ships. Parker took part in another expedition about two weeks later, an expedition exactly like the first. After five months, Parker found a position on another slaver and made his way home to England.[17]

African traders used every means within their power

to control the trade, but English traders were not completely at their mercy. Captains sometimes agreed among
themselves to keep the price of slaves down. Isaac Parker
recalled that a group of captains at Old Calabar placed
themselves under a fifty-pound bond if any of them paid
more than the others for slaves when the African traders
tried to increase the price. The sponsors of a 1762 expedition to Old Calabar instructed the captain, Ambrose
Lace, to make such arrangements; "on your arrival at
Old Callebar if one or more ships be there you will observe to make an agreement with the Master or Masters
so as not to advance the Price on each other and we
doubt not you will use the utmost endeavors to keep
down the Comeys which in Generall are to extravagant
there." The African traders tried to break the cabal by
refusing to sell at the lower price set by the captains. The
captains then put patrols in the river to prevent the Africans from traveling upstream to capture slaves, and they
took anyone they captured as hostages until the traders
agreed to sell slaves at the old, lower price. Captains
might also resort to violence to force the traders to sell
slaves. There were reports of English captains firing
their cannons either into or over the towns in Old Calabar to force traders to the table.[18]

The growth of the slave trade not only increased the
power of the wealthy traders at the expense of traditional leaders whose authority had been based on age
and kinship, but also complicated the relationships be-

tween the towns as they competed for a larger share of the trade. The simple economy based on agriculture, fishing, and trade with the interior was transformed as Old Calabar's economic life came to revolve around the slave trade. The highly profitable slave trade and the ready availability of credit from the Europeans gave the traders access to considerable wealth, which they largely spent on the conspicuous consumption of goods and in amassing an ever larger retinue of slaves, a pattern that led to a highly stratified and unequal social structure sharply divided between free and slave and rich and poor. As in other parts of Africa, control of European trade goods allowed the African elites, in this case the heads of the canoe houses, to convert these goods into "the fundamental values of the African political economy, into dependents and dependency."[19]

The growing wealth from the slave trade and the growth in the number of slaves brought fundamental changes to Efik society. Houses no longer consisted of a related group of freemen and their families, all of them on the same economic footing, growing gradually through natural increase, with wealth and leadership concentrated in the hands of the elders. Instead, houses that grew as a result of the slave trade had only a limited number of freemen with a far larger number of dependents, including larger numbers of slaves, who had been added rapidly and may not have been as fully integrated into the social structure as they would have been previously. As traders grew wealthy on the basis of their abilities rather than rank or age, many freemen who did not prosper from the trade or who belonged to houses left behind in the growing competition became poor and were little better off than servants. Some slaves, on the other hand, prospered and were in the position of masters over their own slaves. But slaves recently purchased from the interior, probably the most rapidly growing segment of the population as the trade expanded, had no rights at all.

Most of the freemen, their servants, their canoe boys and favored slaves, lived in the towns. English sailors were struck by the treatment of household slaves. James Morley, who made many trips to Old Calabar, reported that slaves were treated "with the greatest kindness that I ever have seen." He reported that masters did not sell these slaves; "they do not care to part with such for any price . . . I mean their canoe boys, or house servants." Indeed, it was considered a disgrace, and a mark of poverty, for a master to sell household slaves. Slaves in town provided a wide range of services. Morley observed them "raising provisions, fishing, getting palm-oil, palm-wine, making grass cloths, and other cloth of their own manufacture, making and thatching of houses, going in their canoes backwards and forwards to different places, and attending the necessary duty of their own families and houses." He also remarked that slaves recently imported from the interior were most likely to be employed on the plantations outside the towns, where the introduction of American food crops, especially maize and manioc, greatly increased production and profitability. The importation of European trade goods and the expansion of the slave trade enabled the heads of the canoe houses to increase the number of dependents under their control, for their power continued to be determined by the size of their entourage. With more dependents they could produce more goods, particularly crops for domestic use and for sale to European shippers, and strengthen their own autonomy.[20]

More and more slaves, along with poorer freemen, lived permanently on the plantations. Growing houses greatly expanded the number of plantations under their control to feed the larger number of dependents and to trade with the English ships, which had to buy provisions while they spent months lying at anchor waiting to be slaved. Profits from the sale of provisions to the slave ships could be considerable. Barbot noted that at Old Calabar "we get, in their proper seasons . . . all sorts of eatables, yams, bananas, corn, and other provisions for the slaves." In 1763, for example, Captain James Berry paid Duke Solomon Henshaw 605 coppers for yams, and Antera Duke regularly sold provisions to English captains for substantial sums. The yam trade was vast; captains estimated that it required from 50,000 to 100,000 yams to feed a cargo of 500 slaves during the Middle Passage. Founding new towns and farms in carefully chosen strategic positions along principal waterways gave the chief traders control over important trade routes and greatly increased their supply of foodstuffs and palm oil. Laborers from the plantations could also be brought into town when necessary. Poor freemen, or head men, supervised the large numbers of slaves who worked on the plantations. Here, as in other regions of Africa influenced by the slave trade, Efik slave traders worked within a traditional African economic system based on long-distance trade with the interior through their houses. In keeping with African traditions, they invested most of their profits in dependents, including slaves, and built larger and larger houses. But they also operated within an Atlantic economy; they kept inventories of trade goods, expanded their trade contacts deeper into the interior to acquire more slaves for sale, operated on credit and hard currency, and expanded their commercial activity through the production of agricultural goods for sale to the Europeans.[21] Though still relying on traditional structures, their culture became increasingly commodified.

The establishment of new houses and towns and the growth of the slave-trade economy was accompanied by the need for more effective and centralized governance of society and the trade. The towns became increasingly competitive as the slave trade expanded, and the Efik political system, based on the autonomous lineage houses, lacked any central administration to control these growing tensions. Local kings exercised control over their own towns and conducted negotiations with European slavers, but the slave trade required a more centralized authority capable of exercising some control over these kings and enforcing the peaceful conduct of the trade and payment of debts that the European traders demanded. The Efik traders introduced a complex secret society known as Ekpe (the Efik word for leopard), or Egbo to Europeans. Through the voice of the feared beast, the traders enforced morality, meted out punishments, issued laws that governed all Efiks, forced the payments of debts, and collectively challenged the Europeans. The Ekpe society was not indigenous to Old Calabar, but arose among the Efut, who lived to the east of Old Calabar. According to legend, like good merchants, Efik traders from Old Town purchased the secrets of the society from an Efut man, probably around 1650, just as the slave trade accelerated.[22]

Ekpe introduced a new source of authority into Old Calabar, one firmly controlled by the elite traders and one that held sway over the autonomous towns. Membership was open to all men, including slaves, though only freemen could advance into the highest grades in the society's hierarchy. Entry into each grade had to be bought, so membership in the upper grades was confined to wealthy merchants, who often paid the initiation fees for their free dependents and for their favored slaves. Along with the grades were two prestigious titles, eyamba and ebunko, which could also be bought and were often controlled by a single town or family. Since power within the Ekpe society was exercised from the top down, the elite slave traders controlled it. Each town eventually had its local branch that exercised authority there, but the society's "grand council," composed of the society's powerful traders, made laws that applied to all the traders and towns. The society served several purposes; it helped to integrate the new wards and operated to promote the expansion of the slave trade and related commerce by enforcing the payment of debts, levying fines, impounding property, and imposing trade boycotts on individuals who violated its code.[23]

Through Ekpe, the Efik traders presented a united front to European slavers. For instance, Antera Duke recorded a 1785 incident where a new ship threatened to go to the Cameroons to purchase slaves rather than pay the Old Calabar traders the required comey, which European traders regarded as excessive and higher than the charges imposed elsewhere. "All the gentlemen" met at the home of Egbo Young, a principal trader (who had named his house Liverpool Hall), to discuss the matter. The traders wrote the captain inviting him to come ashore to discuss business, but he refused to leave his ship. Antera Duke and two other principal traders then went on board to negotiate face to face, but the captain still refused to meet their terms, "so we come ashore and tell all the gentlemen, and they say 'Very well, he may go away, please go.'" Duke also records incidences where

African traders "had blown" Ekpe on European traders; blowing Ekpe was one of the most severe Ekpe sanctions because it stopped all trade with them until the dispute was settled. The society punished men who fought with European sailors, ordered traders to replace slaves or pawns who escaped from European slave ships, and otherwise ensured the good conduct of the slave trade. Over time Ekpe spread beyond Old Calabar to include those peoples with whom the Efik had close economic relations, such as the Aro, further facilitating the slave trade.[24]

The Ekpe society's complex rituals and practices helped define Efik social and religious life. The last day of the Efik's eight-day week was sacred to Ekpe. Every town had its Palaver House, a large, low shed with a thatched roof supported by giant mangrove posts. Seats of hardened clay ran the length of the building and one end was enclosed so that the Ekpe's secret ceremonies could be performed in private. In front of the Palaver House hung a great Ekpe drum, fixed on a frame, which was used to signal important events. Ekpe day, or the eighth day of the week, was marked by feast and drink. On that day the feared Ekpe runners scoured the town, masked and dressed in elaborate leopard costumes. The runners carried long whips, and nonmembers of the society remained hidden indoors or suffered lashings at the runners' hands. More elaborate pageantry marked initiation days and other events significant for the society; on these occasions the leopard runners were joined by other runners, some dressed in colorful silks and feathers, some with bows and arrows, followed by musicians, by the great Ekpe drum, and finally by the Ekpe itself, hidden in an ark carried on the shoulders of high officers, who ceremoniously carried the Ekpe into the woods where it was ritually "released" into the bush.

These ceremonies were laden with symbolism; arrows, for instance, represented martial skill, arrows pointed downward represented death, and those pointed upward represented the passage to the other world. This symbolism was also represented by a complex script consisting of over five hundred emblems and ideographs called *nsibidi*. While many symbols were widely recognized, complex ideographs were sacred to ranks within the society and could not be shared even with junior grades. These figures might be displayed on the bodies of Ekpe members, drawn on the ground, engraved on calabashes, woven into fabrics, or exhibited on great cotton banners called *ukara ngbe* cloths.[25]

While drawing on aspects of traditional Efik religion, Ekpe also helped reshape those religious beliefs. The Efik worshiped one god, Abasi, the creator of all things, often referred to as Etenyin Abasi, "our father God," who lived in the sky. The eighth day of the week was sacred to Abasi, and the Efik did not open markets, hunt, fish, or beat drums on that day.[26] They believed that every person had a soul *(ukpon)* which was shared with a particular wild animal (called the "bush soul"); the person shared whatever fate befell the animal. The second day of the week (Auqabibio) was called "prayer day," a day dedicated to the worship of ancestor spirits. Men carried out these ceremonies at a household shrine. Every yard had a small tree, and beside it were human skulls; the shell of a land-turtle hung from the tree, and at the foot of the tree rested one or two basins of water that were never emptied. On prayer day, men poured more water into the basin, called "God's dish," and said prayers to the ancestors. The ceremony might also include the sacrifice of a goat. These vessels carried great symbolism, and Efik slaves who ran away from their masters could claim sanctuary if they broke the god basin.[27] Efik religion was closely tied to place—trees, bodies of water, and other physical features were considered sacred. Supernatural powers known as *ndem*, closely associated with nature and females, could be found in large trees, pools, stone features, and in the Calabar River. Ndem could be worshiped either singly or collectively. Every town had its spirit protector; Anansa, for instance, was the protector of Old Town and lived in a nearby spring or in the Calabar River itself. Occasionally human sacrifices were made to these deities to bring fish to the nets or to encourage the arrival of European slave ships.[28]

The slave trade depended upon a complex marketing system based on credit, governed on the African side by Ekpe, but by long-standing business ties and trust when it came to dealings between English and African traders. Designed to promote personal ties and harmonious relationships, the system did not always function as intended, but it was remarkably effective. Ekpe facilitated commerce, protected the credit arrangements that were more crucial to the trade at Old Calabar than anywhere else in West Africa, and usually prevented the competition between towns from breaking out into open conflict. The Massacre of 1767 was the most glaring example of that failure, but the society became more effective, and more feared, as time passed. Ekpe provided the slave-trading elite with the means to enforce their orders and decisions, and successfully governed individual behavior, including exerting control over the ever-expanding ranks of newly acquired slaves. The commercial aspects of Ekpe were central to the efficient conduct of the slave trade. The society protected the property of its members, adjudicated disputes over debts, and imposed trade boycotts against European traders or Efik towns. For instance, in 1785 Duke Ephraim was summoned before the Ekpe court for his refusal to pay a dept to an English slaver, and was ordered to pay at once. The Ekpe could place individuals under an interdict that prohibited anyone from trading with them, and it could even impose such sanctions on entire towns. By contrast, the Great Duke Ephraim, son of Duke Ephraim, used the society to best his father's old ally, Eyo Nsa (Willy Honesty). Duke Ephraim died in 1786, and his son, known as

the Great Duke Ephraim, built on the foundations his father had laid and carried New Town to a position of
dominance that it never lost. The Great Duke maintained the excellent relations with English traders that his
father had forged and guided Old Calabar from a depen-
dence on slave trading to a position as successful mar-
keter of palm oil in the nineteenth century, a trade he
controlled. The Great Duke brought a serious charge
against Eyo Nsa in the Ekpe court; he alleged that since
Eyo Nsa was not of royal birth he could not be king of
Creek Town. The Great Duke had used his considerable
wealth to buy up all the grades of the Ekpe society, including the eyamba title, one of the two high titles in the
society. Given his control over the society, he was able to
have the Ekpe impose a fine so great that it virtually ru-
ined Eyo Nsa.[29]

In part, a struggle for control over Ekpe may actually
have encouraged the Massacre of 1767, for the society
was initially associated with Old Town, and control over
it became a part of the growing friction between Old
Town and New Town. Grand Epke was the highest title
in the society, and Grandy King George may well have
taken that name when he assumed the top position in the
society. One result of the massacre was to break Old
Town's hold on the society, an outcome that allowed
other slave traders to share its growing power. Evidence
provided by letters from the Old Calabar traders to English merchants in the wake of the massacre demonstrate

that Duke Ephraim and his allies were able to use the Ekpe society to completely crush their Old Town rivals. Grandy King George wrote Ambrose Lace in January 1773 that "the New town peeple . . . blowed abuncko for no ship to go from my water to them nor any to cum from them to me." That this crippling Ekpe sanction was imposed on the king indicates that Old Town had lost control of Ekpe, which then became another weapon in the hands of Duke Ephraim. In 1776 Otto Ephraim, another principal trader at Old Town, wrote Captain Lace that "I please I pay Egbo men yesterday. I have done now for Egbo," which may indicate the final settlement of Ekpe financial sanctions against Old Town. In 1780, King Henshaw joined Duke Ephraim and Eyo Nsa (who signed the letter "Willy Honesty"), the victors of the 1767 massacre, in writing an open letter to the slave traders in Liverpool intended to encourage the traders to return. In the letter, which appeared in the *Liverpool General Advertiser*, they assured the English that "now we make peace . . . No whitemen shall be stop onshor any more long as we be Callabar and we make Great Law about whiteman not hurt. and Suppose one family Stop any whiteman, We will Brock [Break] that family because all Country Stand by that Law this time." By 1780, then, the principal traders could use Ekpe to make "Great Laws" that they could enforce throughout Old Calabar—indeed, by then the elite traders could claim to *be* Calabar.[30] Their boast that they could use their power to "break" a family no doubt referred to their triumph over the Robin Johns.

Ekpe, therefore, had complex and extensive religious, economic, and social authority. More than any other institution, it welded the various Efik towns together and provided a uniform system of government firmly under the control of the slave traders. Almost every conceivable function, from having the streets cleaned to administering justice in criminal cases, fell to Ekpe. In most Ibibio and Ibo communities, only laws accepted at a general council attended by all segments of society were considered valid, but thanks to Ekpe this was not the case among the Efik, where the society made laws that the entire community was bound to respect. The vast power that the society exercised over all of Old Calabar made it essential for everyone who could afford to do so to join the society. Membership dues, along with fines imposed on transgressors, also provided a regular source of income for the elite traders since the money was divided among the members of the highest grade. The Ekpe could impose penalties ranging from fines and boycotts, to arrest and detention, to execution. The Massacre of 1767 indicates that there were important exceptions, particularly when Europeans intervened (as they seldom did), when one town threatened to monopolize the trade, or when the offenders controlled Ekpe (as Old Town did initially). But it is surprising that the intense rivalries between the autonomous towns did not more often erupt into conflict, as occurred elsewhere among slave-trading communities in West Africa, where all-out wars between competing kingdoms or civil wars within slave-trading states could lead to severe disruptions in the trade, a complete collapse of commerce, or the destruction of kingdoms or disintegration of states. In other regions, relations between the European traders and their African counterparts lacked any elements of the trust that under-girded the trade at Old Calabar. On the African coast at Sestos, for example, along the Grain Coast, an ongoing cycle of kidnapping, ransom, and retaliation poisoned relations between English and African traders to the extent that one of the English sailors, John Atkins, noted the "mutual distrust" that existed there.[31]

Trust and close personal relationships between English and African traders were of primary importance, but the slave trade in all its aspects was a brutal business, and violence was never entirely absent from it. In many respects, the Africans at Old Calabar dealt with European traders as equals; they operated within their own market economy, successfully resisted European attempts to monopolize or control their trade, adapted indigenous institutions such as Ekpe to the needs of a commercial economy, and maintained control over their local trading arrangements. Surviving letters between African traders and their English counterparts demonstrate that the English merchants attempted to meet the demands of the local market and even the individual tastes of their African suppliers. The unique aspects of the slave trade at Old

Calabar—the long stays of the English ships in the river, the close personal and economic ties between individual English captains and Efik traders, the creolized society of the literate Old Calabar elite—facilitated close cooperation among these English and Efik merchants.[32] Yet, as the massacre testified, violence and treachery were never precluded.

The rapid changes confronting Efik society after the rise of the Atlantic slave trade were a root cause of the Massacre of 1767. The growth of the canoe houses, the shift in power from the lineage elders to the increasingly rich and influential merchant elite, the population growth and the establishment of new towns, and, most significant, the bitter competition between the towns for the control of the slave trade created a situation where an event like the massacre could occur. The final ingredients in the mix were the presence on the scene of a group of English ship captains intimately aware of the political divisions in Old Calabar and prepared to exploit them by intervening directly and violently in the towns' internal affairs. An alliance between Eyo Nsa and Duke Ephraim to destroy the Robin Johns presented the English captains with an opportunity for cooperation, a degree of cooperation made possible by personal ties, a shared language, and the Efik's willingness to incorporate aspects of English culture into their own. The gracious letters of invitation from English gentlemen to Grandy King George and the gentlemen of Old Town were the necessary first step leading to the downfall of the Robin Johns.

3

"This Deplorable Condition"

The Robin Johns' Enslavement in British America

As Grandy King George nursed his wounds, wrote letters to his old English slave trader friends in search of Little Ephraim and Ancona, and attempted to rebuild his shattered business empire, Little Ephraim and Ancona sweated, retched, and suffered below the stinking decks of the *Duke of York*. Captain Bivins took an estimated 336 captives on board in Old Calabar, and of that number only 272 survived the grueling forty-five–day Middle Passage to be sold on the island of Dominica.[1] It is important to note that the involvement of Africans in the trade did not end on the coast of Africa, but continued during the Middle Passage, where Africans worked as sailors and interpreters on the slave ships. Some of those Africans were enslaved, but many were

hired on the coast of Africa. In addition, sailors often relied on assistants from among the captives as they supervised their cargoes. African sailors from Old Calabar
would play an important role in the Robin Johns' experience in the Americas. The horrors of the Middle Passage
inflicted terrible suffering and traumatized its victims.[2]
Ripped from their homes and families, often marched
long distances to be sold at market, dazed and confused
by the sight of the sea, the slave ships, and Europeans,
most captives had no idea what fate awaited them.

Clearly, the Robin Johns were in a far different position from most victims of the slave trade. Unlike the
vast majority of captives, who were kidnapped in the interior and whose language barriers prevented them from
understanding their plight, the Robin Johns were fully
aware of their predicament. As slave traders, they knew
all too well what lay in store for them. Unlike many captives, they had no fear of the white sailors on board the
Duke of York; in fact, they may well have known some
of them already either from previous voyages or from
their contacts with them while the ship lay at anchor in
the Calabar River off Old Town. If lucky, they may
have found a crewman like John Ashley Hall, whose
duty as second mate was serving the provisions. He
was often on shore in Old Calabar and reported that "I
trusted myself with the natives." He communicated easily with the Efik traders there since "all of them speak
English, some of them very good." Perhaps more impor-

tant for his treatment of the men, women, and children under his supervision, he believed the slave trade to be "perfectly illegal, and founded in blood."[3]

The fact that the two princes were together must have been a tremendous comfort to them, and these young, capable members of the Efik elite were a team bent on survival. Their knowledge of English language and customs was a significant advantage. Many captives suffered for their lack of understanding of the language and customs of the sailors; fear often prevented them from taking offers of assistance from the ship's men, and their refusal to eat brought them severe floggings. John Barbot noted that "all the slaves . . . believe that we buy them to eat them. . . . It is this which makes many slaves die on the passage across, either from sorrow or from despair, there being some who refuse to eat or drink."[4] Whether the Robin Johns' better understanding of their situation made them more or less desperate is impossible to say, but it is certain that they had a more realistic view of their situation than did typical captives. The fact that they were from a slave-trading people gave them a familiarity with the trade, its participants, and its goals. Consequently, we can assume that they had a fundamentally different view of their plight.

It was by no means unheard of for young elite men in Old Calabar to return from long stays abroad, and there were even rare cases of young Efik men who were taken as pawns by English traders, illegally enslaved, sold into slavery in the Americas, and later returned by the slave traders themselves.[5] The surviving letters from Efik traders to their English counterparts indicate that the Efik frequently demanded the return of pawns, usually family members, who had been abducted in violation of usual practice. In 1761, for instance, the English trader William Earle assured Duke Abashy in Old Calabar, "I make no doubt of getting your Boys and Cobham Back . . . for they are all Freemen & No Slaves." It is impossible to know how often traders succeeded in returning such captives, though Captain Lace once purchased a member of an Efik trading family in Jamaica and returned him to Old Calabar, even though the man "was of no consiquance [*sic*] in family." With the bottom line ever in view, Lace reported that "it ansrd [answered] the Expence," no doubt by winning him favor with the man's family.[6] However rare such cases may have been, the Robin Johns knew what most captives did not—that it was possible for them to make their way home. That knowledge, combined with their understanding of English language and customs, must have enabled them to negotiate their enslavement in ways that other captives could not.

Although the Robin Johns left no direct evidence of their voyage, it is possible to reconstruct it from records of other English slave ships. The *Duke of York* was a ship of a hundred tons carrying twelve guns and a crew of forty-five, a modest vessel slightly smaller than the average ship engaged in the trade. Divided by gender, the African captives were crowded onto two decks in the ship's hold specially built by the ship's carpenters for that purpose. Bivins packed the ship more tightly than average, giving each person less than five square feet of deck area. Although there was seemingly no correlation between tight packing and death rates on board slave ships, the death rate of 19 percent on this journey was substantially higher than the average of 14.9 percent on slave voyages from the Bight of Biafra during the period. Death rates were high on voyages from Old Calabar, a fact not lost on sponsors. Investors in a 1762 venture to Old Calabar advised Captain Ambrose Lace that "Callebar is Remarkable for great Mortality in Slaves" and added, "we Desire you may take every Prudent Method to Prevent it."[7]

Coming onto a slave ship was one more step in a process of degradation and dehumanization that began with an individual's capture. Slaves were brought on board with their arms tied behind them with cords. Especially unruly men might be chained together, linked by collars around their necks. The risk of slave uprisings on board was considered greatest during the months that ships spent lying in the Cross River. One captain noted in 1767 that seven vessels were anchored in the river, and that "the major part of the vessels here have very dangerous disorders amongst the slaves, which makes me rejoice that I have very few on board." He also observed that "three captains belonging to Bristol died within these few months, besides a number of officers and sailors." A decimated and weakened crew made an even easier target for rebellion. Captives rose up in revolt in about one in every ten slaving voyages, though voyages from the Bight of Biafra showed a lower incidence of revolts than those from other regions. In a bitter play on the biblical creation story, sailors called the first male captive brought on board Adam and the first female Eve. Men were stripped naked and locked in irons during the entire voyage, the right leg of one man locked to the left leg of another. Women were generally not locked in irons and might be given strips of cloth to cover themselves. Being bound together created great difficulties for the men and often resulted in fights and arguments. As one sailor reported, "They frequently disagree in the night about their sleeping places; and frequently the men linked together disagree and fight, when one wants perhaps to obey the calls of nature, and the other has been unwilling to go with him." No doubt their tempers became increasingly frayed as the journey continued. Captains resorted to the most extreme measures to prevent those tensions from erupting into rebellion. One captain advised that if an uprising occurred, "spare no effort to repress their insolence and as an example to the others, sacrifice the lives of all the most mutinous. . . . The way of making it clear to them, I mean the form of punishment that scares Africans most, is by chopping parts off a living man with blows from an axe and presenting the separated parts to the others." With high mortality rates, suicides, dismemberments, and executions, it is no surprise that hungry sharks trailed the bloody slave ships across the Atlantic.[8]

Food on board the ships was often meager, though some captains tried to accommodate the slaves' food preferences in an attempt to lessen mortality rates during the Middle Passage. Barbot noted that he tried to supply slaves with food they liked, "the Calabar slaves being generally better pleas'd with food of their own country, than with any of Europe." Slaves received a steady diet of beans, rice, and yams with a bit of palm oil and pepper for seasoning. Many slaves fell into a state of depression and refused to eat, and they often suffered for their obstinacy. Sailors referred to this condition as "sulking" and resorted to extreme measures to compel slaves to eat. Sailors might first simply strike slaves with their fists, but when that failed they often resorted to a cat-o'-nine-tails, a whip made of nine knotted leather cords attached to a wooden handle. More difficult cases brought more extreme measures. A sailor named George Millar told the story of "a woman Slave being brought on board . . . who refused any sustenance, neither would she speak: she was at last ordered to have thumb-screws put upon her, and suspended in the mizen rigging, and every attempt made by the cat and those instruments they generally have on board the ships, but all to no purpose; she died three or four days after that, and I was told by some of the women Slaves that she spoke to some of them the night before she died, and said, 'She was going to her friends.'" John Barbot confessed that "I must say I am naturally compassionate, yet have I been necessitated sometimes to cause the teeth of those wretches to be broken, because they would not open their mouths, or be prevail'd upon by any intreaties to feed themselves; and thus have forced some sustenance into their throats." In later years slave ships were furnished with an instrument called a speculum oris, invented to pry open the mouths of lockjaw victims, to force open the mouths of "sulky" captives. Some slaves took their own lives because they believed that if they died their souls would return to Africa.[9]

Traders believed that exercise was necessary to keep the captives healthy. Slaves were brought above decks to take meals, and after each meal they were compelled "to jump up and down upon the beating of a drum." The rolling of the ship made such exercise difficult, and male slaves were further constrained by the shackles. Perhaps for that reason, men more often refused to participate than women. When captives would not do the "dance," as the exercise was called, then sailors forced them with the cat-o'-nine-tails. Along with drummers, some slave ships employed bagpipers, though whether they were intended to entertain the crew or the slaves is unclear.[10]

Since the ships sailed through tropical seas, the heat

caused great suffering. One sailor reported that "I have frequently heard them crying out when below for the want of air; and between decks of an African ship with their Slaves on board, it is so violently hot, that I have frequently, after being below but a few minutes, had my shirt so wet by perspiration, that I could have wrung it as if it had been steeped in water." Slave ships generally had gratings in the decks to allow air to flow below, and many others were fitted with air ports along the side of the ship to funnel more fresh air below the decks. The situation below became more desperate during storms, when the grates had to be covered with tarpaulins. Women, who had more freedom of movement than men, often crawled onto the ship's beams to get closer to the gratings, but when sailors found them there they forced them back down into the decks. The ports were also closed at night because the English believed that "the night Air is very Pernicious."[11]

Slave ships leaving Old Calabar often stopped in the Cape Verde Islands to replenish their supplies of food and especially of fresh water. The trip to Porto Praya (Praia), the port of St. Jago (Sao Tiago) island, took about three weeks. Porto Praya would be the last sight of land until the ship reached the Caribbean, some four weeks later if sailing conditions were good.[12]

The threat of slave uprisings was ever present, and as a result slave ships carried larger crews than ships engaged in other forms of commerce. The forty-five sailors aboard the *Duke of York* worked under harsh conditions. In fact, the trade was so notorious among sailors that captains resorted to a variety of ruses to assemble a crew. For instance, captains in port cities like Bristol often worked with landlords whose tenants fell into debt and could not pay their rent. Landlords gave them the choice of joining the crew of a Guineaman or going to debtors prison. Captains often took poor boys of nine or ten as apprentices, paying little or nothing for their services. James Morley of Bristol recalled that he first joined the crew of a slave ship at the age of nine or ten as a servant. Over the years, he was gradually promoted to gunner, boatswain, and, finally, mate. Despite ill-usage, he recalled that he remained in the trade for several years because of "a promise of promotion, and to maintain my family, having been brought up in that trade at that time." He reported that seamen on Guineamen were treated "with great rigour, and many with cruelty." Some officers were physically abusive. One Matthews, the chief mate on the *Venus,* "would knock a man down for a very frivolous thing; such as not being as quick as he wanted him with a swab, or upon any small occasion, and this, with any thing he could get in his hand, a cat, a piece of wood, or a cook's ax, with which he once cut a man down his right shoulder, by throwing of this ax at him in his passion." Such violence was by no means unusual. Provisions on the ships were usually scanty, and since the holds were filled to capacity with slaves and supplies, sailors had no choice but to sleep on the decks. As Morley put it, sailors had no shelter but "the heavens, none that I know of; in the Middle Passage . . . they lie upon deck and die upon deck: that I have seen." As a result of poor diet and exposure to infection, disease was common. Many sailors contracted tropical diseases, especially malaria and water-borne diseases, while their ships lay, often for months, at anchor in the Cross River, waiting for the slaves to be purchased and delivered.[13]

Many desperate sailors deserted the slave ships once they reached the West Indies, where the slaves were offloaded, and captains often discharged sick seamen once the ships docked. For example, of the 940 crewmen on twenty-four Bristol Guineamen in 1787, 216 died and another 239 either deserted or were discharged in the colonies. The ships required fewer sailors as they made their way from the West Indies back to England, and captains and owners were eager to reduce costs by discharging as many men as possible. As a further cost-cutting measure, sailors were often paid all or part of their wages in the debased currency of the islands rather than in sterling. Known by such names as wharfingers and beach horners, the sick sailors could be found "lying about the wharfs, beaches, and different places, in almost all the islands of the West Indies, with ulcerated legs and other disorders, almost dead." These men suffered from scurvy or black scurvy, the most dreaded illness that plagued sailors engaged in the slave trade. John Ashley Hall, who began his career as a crewman but was eventually promoted to captain, reported mortality rates as high as 68 percent for crewmen on slave ships. Figures from Liverpool ships in the 1770s reveal a mortality rate of 28 percent for slave ship crews during the Middle Passage, a rate that soared to 45 percent while ships remained on the African coast. The high death rate among slaves on board the *Duke of York* suggests that the crew also suffered a high mortality rate. When diseases struck the African captives, they often spread to the crew as well, especially to those men who had direct contact with the Africans. Hall recalled that "the crews of the African ships, when they arrive in the West Indies, are generally in a sickly debilitated state, and they seamen who are discharged or desert from those ships . . . are they most miserable objects I ever met with in any country in my life; I have frequently seen them with their toes rotted off, their legs swelled to the size of their thighs, and in an ulcerated state all over." He believed the slave trade "to be particularly destructive to the seamen employed in it, and beyond every degree of comparison with any trade I am acquainted with."[14]

After several weeks at sea, Captain Bivins sailed the *Duke of York* into harbor at Dominica. He may have gone directly to Roseau, the island's principal city, though a high surf sometimes made docking there difficult. At times, ships anchored some thirty feet offshore, then placed two long joists, called skids, over the boat's stern that reached to the shore. Goods, and people, could then be moved on and off the ship. It is more likely that the ship docked at Woodbridge Bay, "the general place where all Guinea-men in particular bring up on their arrival." The bay was only a short distance from Roseau, but the water was smoother there and the low surf permitted ships to load and unload their cargoes more safely.[15]

The details of the Robin Johns' enslavement on Dominica are sketchy, but the limited evidence suggests that they were more savvy than most men in their circumstances. Like many of the islands in the Lesser Antilles, Dominica had bounced from one European nation to another as the colonial powers struggled for dominance in the Caribbean. For many years Dominica was a French colony like its nearest neighbors, Martinique and Guadeloupe, but the British acquired the island in 1763 as a part of the Treaty of Paris. A British free port, Roseau attracted Frenchmen and Spaniards from nearby Caribbean islands who bought slaves and British manufactured goods there, while American traders brought lumber, foodstuffs, cattle, and other goods to supply Caribbean sugar planters. The island had a sugar and coffee plantation system of its own. Production on Dominica received a boost after a 1727 earthquake severely decreased production on Martinique and thus caused a mass exodus of over a thousand planters to Dominica and the small French island of Alourzie. Acquisition by the British brought another boom fueled by high prices for sugar and coffee. The English commissioner of lands reported that "since our conquest of Jamaica from the Spaniards, in the days of Oliver Cromwell, down to the present times, there has been no such opportunity of improving private fortunes." Hungry investors rushed to purchase land and open plantations. The importation of slaves reflected the island's rapid expansion; fewer than a hundred were imported in 1765, but over 3,500 came three years later when the Robin Johns arrived.[16]

Slaves were sold either on the ship or on the shore, most often on the shore. Government officials often got the first pick of slaves aboard the ships before they were unloaded and offered for general sale. The ship's captain negotiated the price for each slave sold and did his best to obtain the highest possible price. Slaves who were ill or infirm often could not be sold through individual purchases; they were known as "refuse slaves" and were offered at auction or "vendue," where they sold for only a few dollars. Another common form of sale was known as the "scramble," for reasons that the following description makes clear:

The ship was darkened with sails, and covered round. The men slaves were placed on the main deck, and the women on the quarter deck. The purchasers on shore were informed a gun would be fired when they were ready to open the sale. A great number of people came on board with tallies or cards in their hands, with their own names upon them, and rushed through the barricado door with the ferocity of brutes. Some had three or four handkerchiefs tied together, to encircle as many as they thought fit for the purpose.

The fact that the Robin Johns remained together suggest that they were sold by individual purchase. Did Captain Bivins make a special effort to keep them together? It could be that the men made themselves useful on the voyage and found favor with the captain. Often, Africans on board the ships were appointed "quartermasters." They assisted in organizing their fellow captives at mealtimes, supervised the work crews that cleaned the lower decks, and reported any threat of rebellion. They were rewarded with special treatment that might include more food, more clothing, and other privileges. Given the Robin Johns' language skills and their own experience as slave traders, they would have been ideal candidates for that position.[17]

Slave traders usually made no effort to keep families together, not even mothers and children, much less brothers. The Robin Johns, however, not only survived, but were sold together to a French physician who treated them relatively well. There can be little doubt that the princes' higher level of acculturation made it possible for them to avoid a more terrible fate. Ancona later wrote that "we was treated according to what they could make

of us upon ye whole not badly." The doctor probably
practiced in Roseau, a rollicking city bustling with Englishmen, Frenchmen, Spaniards, Genoese, and island-
born creoles. The Robin Johns' ability to communicate
in English must have been a valuable asset given the island's recent change of hands, and their knowledge of
African languages would have been a great advantage as
well. Most of the slaves on Dominica were fairly recent
arrivals, and well over half of the 37,873 known to have
been imported between 1751 and 1775 came from the
Bight of Biafra. Their relatively benign treatment under-
scores Ira Berlin's point that "if slavery meant abuse and
degradation, the experience of Atlantic creoles provided
strategies for limiting such maltreatment."[18]

Dominica's mountainous terrain and irregular and un-
guarded coastline invited smuggling, as did its reputation
as a free-wheeling port. Smuggling was so common that
it became "part of the accepted order of things" on the
island. Seven months after the Robin Johns' arrival, Captain William Sharp of Liverpool sailed the *Peggy* into the
harbor at Roseau, on one of his many voyages carrying
cargoes of slaves from the Windward Coast, an important slave-trading region in modern-day Liberia and Sierra Leone. The captain was no stranger to the smuggling common on Dominica, and he somehow learned
about the Robin Johns and promised to return them to
Africa if they could make their way on board his ship.
Ancona and Little Ephraim, in their own words, "were

determined to get home," and they managed to escape to Sharp's sloop in the dark of night. The unscrupulous captain had no intention of returning them to Old Calabar. His ship was bound not for Africa, but for Virginia, where Sharp sold Ancona and Little Ephraim into slavery.[19]

Once again these Atlantic creoles avoided the drudgeries of plantation labor and even managed to remain together. Sharp sold them to Captain John Thompson in Virginia. Thompson, a native of Bristol, operated a store in Williamsburg in partnership with John and James Tarpley until 1766, when he advertised the store for sale. Thompson apparently relocated to York County, Virginia, where he traded between Virginia and Bristol. He owned at least one schooner and often took the Robin Johns to sea with him. The princes were not as fortunate in their treatment, however, as they had been with the Dominican physician. Captain Thompson was abusive, and Ancona recalled that "he would tie me up & whip me many times for nothing at al[l] then some times be Cause I could not Dress his Diner for him not understanding how to do it . . . he was exceeding badly man ever I saw."[20]

Despite their mistreatment, the Robin Johns may well have been fortunate to find themselves on the ship. As Paul Gilroy wrote, ships were "micro-systems of linguistic and political hybridity," an ideal environment for Atlantic creoles such as the Robin Johns. Black sailors were by no means unusual on eighteenth-century ships, and skilled watermen like the Robin Johns brought their knowledge of boats with them from Africa. Guineamen often employed skilled African sailors, whom they hired on the African coast. Captains sometimes attempted to enslave them, but the rights of these free sailors were upheld in the English courts. In 1779 Chief Justice Lord Mansfield awarded Amissa, a free black sailor from Anamaboe, a slave-trading port on the Gold Coast, £500 in damages in a suit involving the captain of a Liverpool ship. The captain had hired Amissa on the African coast in 1774 and paid him part of his wages in advance. When the slave ship reached Jamaica, however, the captain sold Amissa into slavery and later told his relatives that he had died on the Middle Passage. Years later, another black sailor from Anamaboe reported that Amissa was still alive and enslaved. His relatives then persuaded another captain to redeem him. Amissa was taken to London, where he won his case and returned home. Slaveowners in the Americas recognized the skills of African sailors such as Amissa and exploited them. The historian W. Jeffrey Bolster noted that "enslaved black sailors established a visible presence in every North American seaport and plantation roadstead between 1740 and 1865." Like other skilled slaves, sailors enjoyed greater independence than most field hands, and their wide travels made them among the best-informed men in the slave community. They also had more opportunities to escape than most slaves. About 25 percent of the skilled runaways in Virginia between 1736 and 1801 were sailors.[21]

In March 1772, the *Virginia Gazette* printed the following announcement: "Friday last died . . . Captain Thompson, on board the schooner George, from Virginia." To the Robin Johns, who were aboard the ship when their owner collapsed after complaining of a stomach ache, it appeared that providence had once again intervened on their behalf. After several years of abuse at Thompson's hands, they were relieved but frightened when the captain suddenly fell dead while walking along the deck. His death gave them another opportunity to make their escape.[22]

About three weeks after Thompson's death, a ship called the *Greyhound* arrived in Virginia under the command of Captain Terence O'Neil. A Bristol Guineaman, the ship had left England for Old Calabar in 1772, carried 132 slaves to South Carolina, and then sailed to Virginia. In one of the remarkable coincidences in the Robin Johns' story, two African sailors employed on board the *Greyhound* were from Old Calabar; they recognized the Robin Johns and knew the details of their capture. At their urging, O'Neil sent for Little Ephraim and promised to buy him and Ancona, but it soon became evident that he did not have the money to do so. Instead, he offered to return them to Old Calabar on his next voyage out of Bristol if they would run away at night and board his ship. Once again they made a daring escape.[23] Safely on board the *Greyhound* with men from Old Calabar who could give them information about their families and friends, the Robin Johns dreamed of returning home at last as the ship made its way across the Atlantic.

4

"We Were Free People"

Bristol, the English Courts, and the Question of Slavery

When the *Greyhound* arrived in Bristol, O'Neil left Ancona and Little Ephraim on board and promised to transfer them to an outbound ship for the trip to Africa. He did have them transferred to another ship, the *Brickdale*, commanded by William Wood and owned by Henry Lippincott, but it was not bound for Africa. Instead, the ship was headed back to Virginia. They quickly realized that they had been tricked again by an unscrupulous captain who planned to sell them back into slavery. Little Ephraim described their "great surprise & horror" when they discovered that they had been duped once more. He and Ancona were devastated "when the[y] came to put on the Irons[,] we then with tears and trembling began to pray to God to helpe us in this Deplorable condition." The *Brickdale* was lying at Kingroad, an anchorage near the mouth of the Avon used by ships, especially those in the colonial trade, too large to sail upriver to Bristol.[1]

Once again, though their situation looked bleak, the Robin Johns were lucky, extremely fortunate that the *Greyhound* had brought them to Bristol, a hub of the eighteenth-century Atlantic World and one of the most important slave-trading ports in England, where their status as scions of an elite slave-trading family of Old Calabar proved to be their salvation. The *Greyhound* would probably have tied up at the Quay, about a mile long, a bustling, noisy center of commerce surrounded by ships, merchants' countinghouses, shops and warehouses, refineries, and the indispensable taverns and coffeehouses that served the sailors and captains. All the vast commerce of England's colonial empire arrived at the Quay; ships unloaded their New World cargoes of sugar, rum, tobacco, iron, fish, and other products, and from Europe and the Mediterranean came wine, brandy, cloth, timber, and other goods. Bristol's Atlantic trade more than doubled in the eighteenth century. Its narrow, crowded, dirty streets bustled with activity; its citizens were "all in a hurry, running up and down with cloudy looks and busy faces, loading, carrying, and unloading goods and merchandises of all sorts . . . for the trade of many nations is drawn hither." Even the clergy, it was said, "talk of nothing but trade and how to turn a penny."[2]

The eighteenth century was Bristol's golden age, the height of the city's wealth and influence as a major Atlantic port, a status gained in large part through the profits of the slave trade. Bristol merchants moved into the trade after the Royal African Company lost its monopoly in 1698. From that date until the abolition of the trade in 1807, at least 2,114 slave ships left Bristol, almost 20 percent of all British voyages. Bristol merchants invested approximately £150,000 annually in the slave trade at its peak (or over $10,500,000 in today's dollars). Contemporaries noted the enormous importance of the trade to the city; in the words of one writer, there was "not a brick in the city but what is cemented with the blood of a slave." By the 1740s Bristol had ceded its position as the leading slave port to Liverpool, but the trade remained important. Slaving ventures were expensive, and Bristol merchants such as Thomas Jones and Ambrose Lace usually formed ad hoc partnerships to finance individual voyages. The number of partners on a venture might range from two to ten, but the reliance on these networks among a relatively small and highly specialized number of slave traders meant that the personal ties between them were unusually close.[3]

The fact that this small, closely knit group of English slave traders had formed close personal relationships with their Efik counterparts in Old Calabar enabled the Robin Johns to find a most unlikely savior. Rallying from their shock, they searched for a solution to their latest dilemma. After almost two weeks locked in the "writched [wretched] transport," Little Ephraim wrote Thomas Jones, a veteran slave trader with a long association with the Robin Johns at Old Town, the same man to whom Grandy King George and Orrock Robin John had written immediately after Little Ephraim and Acnona were abducted. Jones, who began his career as a crewmen on Guineamen, had been trading for slaves at Old Town since the 1750s. Jones was a propitious choice; one of the most prominent slavers in the city, he, along with his partner James Jones, controlled about 40 percent of the tonnage of African vessels leaving Bristol by late 1700s.[4] Here again their experience as slave traders and the personal ties they had established in Old Calabar served them well. In 1760 and 1763 Jones had made slave-trading voyages to Old Town, where he had met Little Ephraim and Ancona, "they having been several times on board" his ship "delivering messages for, and other times accompanying one Grandee Ephraim Robin John upon commercial transactions."[5] The fact that they were able to write Jones is strong evidence that the Robin Johns had won friends among the crewmen on the ship where they were being held; how else could they have gotten writing materials and had their letters mailed or delivered to Jones?

Jones did not respond to their first letter, which "made Anconas heart fill," but Little Ephraim wrote a second time. Again, Jones did not answer and the *Brickdale* was about to set sail, "but the Lord was good [and] stayed the wind which prevented our sail then I write agin to Mr. Jones wch moved him to pity." Attempting to find more information about the men, Jones first turned to his fellow slave trader Ambrose Lace, one of the captains involved in the Massacre of 1767. Lace had brought another young member of the Old Town elite, "young Ep[rai]m" (Robin John Otto Ephraim), to Liverpool after the massacre in 1767. Lace schooled the boy in England for two years before returning him to Old Town, in hopes of establishing good relations in the future. The stratagem worked, and Lace maintained a long and mutually profitable relationship with Robin John Otto Ephraim after he returned to Old Calabar and became a prominent slave trader in his own right. Jones wrote Lace to try to persuade him to submit an affidavit in support of his effort to free the men. In his response, Lace reviewed the genealogy of the Robin family in some detail. As he reported, "I have several times had the pedigree of all the familys from Abashey [another prominent trader in Old Calabar]." He expressed doubts that Little Ephraim and Ancona were who they claimed to be; "but to prove the two men to be Epms. [Ephraim's] brothers I don't know how you will do it, I assure you I don't think they are." Lace explained that "Old Robin took Rob.

Rob. Jno. mother for a wife when Robin Rob. Jno. was a boy of 6 or eight years old, and as to Rob. Rob. Jno. he never had a son that I heard of. You know very well the custom of that place whatever Man or Woman gos to live in any family they take the Name of the first man in the family and call him Father, how little Epm. came into the family I cant tell, and as to what ship they came off the coast in I know no more than you, therefore can't make Affadavit." He also heaped scorn on Grandy King George; "as to Grandy Epm.," he wrote, "you know very well [he] has been Guilty of many bad Act[i]ons, no man can say anything in his favour, a History of his life would exceed any of our Pirates, the whole sett at Old Town you know as well as me." Lace added, "if you think to send a vessell to Old Town it might ansr [answer] for you to purchas[e] the two men."[6]

Lace knew far more about Little Ephraim and Ancona than he was willing to admit. Grandy King George wrote Lace in 1773 and listed many members of his family, including two of his sons and the sons of "Robbin" and "the King of Qua," who had been abducted. It is likely that Little Ephraim and Ancona were the sons of "Robbin" alluded to in the letter. There can also be little doubt that Lace knew of their capture by Captain Bivins; it was common knowledge among the slave traders and certainly among those involved in the Massacre of 1767. The arrival of the Robin Johns in England and Jones's efforts to free them raised the troubling issue of the massacre, something that Lace was eager to avoid. He was aware that Jones had already located a sailor named William Floyd, chief mate on the *Indian Queen* during the massacre, who gave an extremely detailed and damning affidavit about the bloody event and Lace's role in it. Lace dismissed Floyd's testimony as a pack of lies and charged that "he says more then I ever knew or heard of . . . a man should be careful when on Oath . . . ," a warning that Lace himself would have cause to remember as Jones prepared to bring the entire matter to trial.[7]

The Robin Johns' case was an important one in the legal history of slavery in England, coming as it did on the heels of the famous *Somerset* case. In 1772 Chief Justice Lord Mansfield ruled that James Somerset, who had been brought to England as a slave but had escaped from his master, could not be reenslaved and returned to Jamaica. Somerset's case was similar to the Robin Johns' in several respects.[8] Somerset was owned by Charles Stewart, who had purchased him in Virginia and brought him to London. After two years, Somerset ran away from his master, but he was recaptured and imprisoned on a ship outbound for Jamaica, where Stewart planned to sell his rebellious servant. Somerset's friends quickly gathered affidavits about his case and presented them to Lord Mansfield, who granted a writ of habeus corpus against the captain of the ship where Somerset was being held. The writ ordered the captain to bring Somerset before Mansfield at his London chambers. Mansfield attempted to settle the matter out of court, but when that failed, he ordered the case to trial. The trial opened in February 1772 and aroused considerable attention; every meeting of the court was crowded with onlookers, including a black delegation. Mansfield handed down his ruling in June 1772. The Chief Justice of the King's Bench ruled that "the state of slavery is of such a nature, that it is incapable of being . . . introduced . . . upon mere reasoning, . . . natural or political; it must take its rise from . . . *positive law* long after all traces of the occasions, reasons, authority, and *time of its introduction,* are lost, and in a case so odious . . . We cannot say, the cause set forth by this return is allowed or approved by the laws of this kingdom, and therefore the man must be discharged."[9]

Almost immediately the English press reported that Mansfield's ruling outlawed slavery in England, a misconception that has persisted to the present. In fact, the conservative justice did not intend to hand down such a sweeping decision. Widely regarded as a champion of commercial law, Mansfield was greatly concerned about the effects of his ruling on property rights. He commented that "the setting of 14,000 or 15,000 men [the estimated number of enslaved blacks in England at the time] at once loose by a solemn opinion, is very disagreeable in the effects it threatens." Mansfield had firsthand knowledge of the presence of blacks in England; his mulatto grand-niece, Dido Elizabeth Lindsay, lived with him as part of the family. He confirmed her freedom in his will and left her a substantial settlement. Despite the presence of a black woman in his own family, Mansfield hesitated to issue a ruling that questioned the legality of slavery and crafted as narrow a ruling as he could. For Mansfield, the case hinged on questions of work discipline, property, and personal rights and obligations. He focused solely on the question of whether or not a master could forcibly send his slave outside the country against the slave's will. In a carefully constructed decision, Mansfield turned to a 1679 law that forbade the deportation of subjects and residents of the kingdom (aside from those deported in criminal cases) against their will, and on that basis ruled that Somerset could not be forced to leave England. The case did not settle the larger questions surrounding the legality of slavery in England. Mansfield himself stressed that point a few years later when he wrote that "there had been no determination that they [slaves] were free, the judgement went no further than to determine the Master had no right to compel the slave to go into a foreign country." The justice's hesitancy was not lost on contemporaries, including Benjamin Franklin, then in London, who heaped scorn "on the hypocrisy of this country, which encourages such a detestable commerce by laws for promoting the Guinea trade; while it piqued itself on its virtue, love of liberty, and the equity of its courts, in setting free a single negro." Subsequent events proved that Franklin's skepticism was well founded.[10]

As narrow as the *Somerset* case was, it could easily be applied to the case of the Robin Johns. Still, Henry Lippincott, owner of the *Brickdale*, and William Jones, the agent for the Virginia owners, refused to release them unless they were paid £80 for each of them. Thomas Jones clearly appealed to the *Somerset* ruling in his attempt to free the Robin Johns by writ of habeas corpus. Jones argued that the Robin Johns were being held prisoner "in order to be conveyed out of this Kingdom to Virginia against their consent and in order to be made Slaves." The court apparently agreed and handed down the writ, and the Robin Johns left the *Brickdale*, but their ordeal was far from over. They were provided with a carriage, which drove them the five miles from Kingroad to Bristol and pulled up in front of Henry Lippincott's door. When the Robin Johns stepped out of the carriage, they were confronted by a bailiff and one or two other men waiting for them at the door. The bailiff arrested the bewildered men and carried them first to a "Lock-up House and afterwards to the House of Correction." In yet another twist in the complex case, Captain Terence O'Neil, the captain who had brought them from Virginia to England, had the Robin Johns arrested for "a pretended Debt for their said passage to England"![11]

Little Ephraim again took matters into his own hands and wrote Lord Mansfield, who, in Little Ephraim's words, "send to fetch us to London where we was examined then Discharged." Mansfield wanted to examine the princes in person, just as he had James Somerset.[12] Little Ephraim's literacy and his clever manipulation of the English legal system exemplify the importance of the Atlantic creoles' remarkable skills and understanding of the wider Atlantic World. Little Ephraim's grasp of the significance of Mansfield's ruling raises the possibility that he had heard of it before leaving Virginia. In a 1773 advertisement, a Virginia slaveowner who was searching for runaways from his plantation said, "I have some Reason to believe they will endeavor to get out of the Colony, particularly to Britain, where they imagine they will be free (a Notion now too prevalent among the Negroes, greatly to the Vexation and Prejudice of the Masters) I hereby forewarn Masters of Vessels from carrying them off at their Peril." The news of the *Somerset* case raised such hopes. And news that kept alive hopes of freedom would quickly have spread through the extensive communication networks among blacks in the Atlantic World, and especially via "maritime maroons" such as the Robin Johns, who played an important role in conveying information from one port to another.[13]

Little Ephraim's gamble paid off, but the arrival of his letter perplexed Lord Mansfield. Despite the similarities in the Somerset and Robin John cases, there were significant differences. There was no question that Somerset was a slave, but with the Robin Johns the matter was not so clear. Indeed, the Robin Johns argued in their deposition to Mansfield that they were freemen:

when we first went on board Captain Bevan's [*sic*] ship, we were free people, and no ways subject to the people of New Town; nor had they any right or power over us; nor were we conquered in fight or battle, or taken prisoners by them; nor had they any right to sell us . . . we had not done anything to forfeit our liberty; or had the people of New Town any right or power over us; nor had the English captains (as we understood and verily believe) any right to assist the people of New Town, if they and the people of Old Town had actually engaged in fight or battle, whilst the English captains were present. But there was no war between the people of New Town and the people of Old Town, but only a quarrel or dispute about trade, which never occasioned any fighting.[14]

Here we have the remarkable case of African slaves arguing to the Lord Chief Justice of England that their enslavement violated the rules governing the Efik slave trade and English law as well. As we have already seen, when Dick Ebro asked Isaac Parker to go on a slave-raiding expedition when him, he said, "Parker, will you go to war with me?" Efik traders kept up the pretense that even their most blatant slave raids were actually engagements in warfare, and they were carried out against their traditional enemies. The Massacre of 1767 was not a war, and the Robin Johns rightly argued that they had never been defeated in battle or taken prisoner by the men from New Town. They had been taken prisoner by Captain Bivins, who had no more right to capture them than had the residents of New Town. It was the same argument their father made to Thomas Jones in his 1767 letter when he identified them as "free Men," a status that was every bit as important in Old Calabar as in any slave-holding society. As princes of Old Town, they certainly had never been sold by anyone who could reasonably claim to be their owner. After the massacre was over, the English captains involved in it held several "meetings and consultations," in which they decided to make token payments of a few coppers to the traders from New Town for the Old Town captives they intended to enslave. By making these payments, far below the market value of slaves at the time, the captains hoped "to give the Transaction some sort of Colour or Appearance of an fair Trade, in case they should, on their return to England, be called to an account for having violated the Acts of Parliament for regulation the Trade to Africa." When it came to parsing law, the Robin Johns proved themselves almost as expert as the Lord Chief Justice himself, who agreed that the case hinged on the issues they presented: Had they been legitimately enslaved? Mansfield also noted that "the whole transaction was beyond sea"—outside England and its dominion—which complicated the matter of jurisdiction in the case.[15]

An additional complication involved the chain of

ownership of the Robin Johns. Even if they had been legally enslaved and sold in Dominica, they had run away, or rather they had been stolen by Captain William Sharp, and sold illegally to Captain Thompson in Virginia. While Mansfield noted that Thompson had made "a fair purchase," it was equally clear that Sharp did not have legal title. Here again, Mansfield had heard an earlier case that bore directly on this question. In *Lewis v. Stapylton*, Robert Stapylton was tried for kidnaping Thomas Lewis, whom he claimed as his slave. Stapylton had owned Lewis, but the slave had been captured by the crew of a Spanish ship, had thereafter lived as a freeman, and had worked for wages in various colonies. Lewis was living as a freeman in Chelsea when Stapylton and two other men "in a dark night seized the person of Lewis, and, after a struggle, dragged him . . . into a boat lying in the Thames, where, having first tied his legs, they endeavour[ed] to gag him, by thrusting a stick into his mouth; and then rowing down to a ship bound for Jamaica, whose commander was previously engaged in the wicked conspiracy, they put him on board, to be sold for a slave on his arrival in the island." The ship's departure was delayed by unfavorable winds, and that delay allowed time for a writ of habeas corpus to be served. The case came before Lord Mansfield and a jury in February 1771. Reluctant to make any rulings about the law in general, Mansfield asked the jury to decide if Lewis was indeed Stapylton's property. He left the possibility open that masters might well prove such ownership since "whether they have this kind of property or not, in England, has never been solemnly determined." Mansfield told the jury that if they found that Lewis was indeed Stapylton's property they should arrive at a special verdict which would open up "a more solemn discussion concerning the right of such property in England." Mansfield breathed an obvious sigh of relief when the jury found that since Lewis had been captured by a Spanish privateer and removed from Stapylton's control, the chain of ownership had been broken, that Lewis was not Stapylton's property, and could not be reenslaved. Mansfield ended the proceedings by observing, "I don't know what the consequences may be, if the masters were to lose their property by accidentally bringing their slaves to England. I hope it never will be finally discussed; for I would have all masters think them free, and all Negroes think they were not, because then they would both behave better." Certainly that case presented another possible argument for freeing the Robin Johns. No more eager to make a clear ruling on the legitimacy of slavery in England than he had been before, the Chief Justice confronted a real conundrum and confessed that he "thought the case was not without difficulty."[16]

Even as Mansfield was scratching his powdered wig over the complexities of the case, negotiations were under way in Bristol between the various parties. On November 6, 1773, the defendants asked for a ten-day delay, and a week later they announced a compromise. Recall that Ambrose Lace had suggested to Jones that he should consider purchasing the two men, and apparently the agent for the Virginia claimants was also willing to consider such an arrangement. That may have offered the easiest resolution, but it was not one that Jones was willing to pursue. Perhaps he felt he had the stronger case, or perhaps he thought the illegal enslavement of the brothers was worthy of notice. It does not appear that the Robin Johns were the reluctant parties; they offered to exchange ten slaves for their freedom. Their family members made similar offers for their return. The Efik slave traders often gave such compensation to the English captains who retrieved their lost family members, not as any form of purchase but rather to offset the trouble and expense involved in returning them.[17]

In a surprising turn of events, it was James Bivins, the captain who had captured the Robin Johns in Old Calabar, who was forced to pay £120 to the alleged owners in Virginia as "purchase money or value of the said two Africans." Additionally, Captain O'Neil gave up his transparent claim that the men should be held for debt. The compromise was not simply a private matter; the details of the agreement were submitted to the court and formally accepted.[18] That fact raises the likelihood that Mansfield himself had played some part in those negotiations; if so, that could explain why Bivins agreed to pay after six years. Mansfield usually tried to get such cases settled out of court. Clearly, Bivins was unwilling to face the Robin Johns in Mansfield's court, where the bloody details of the Massacre of 1767 would be laid before the bench and the public. It may also be that the closely knit slave traders in Bristol, who had their own reasons for not wanting to have the case heard given the actions of the captains in the massacre, brought pressure to bear on him. The intriguing possibilities behind the compromise aside, Little Ephraim and Ancona walked out of jail in Bristol as the freemen they so adamantly claimed to be.

5

"A Very Blessed Time"

The Robin Johns and English Methodism

When Little Ephraim and Ancona found themselves locked in irons on board the *Brickdale* contemplating a return to enslavement in Virginia, "with tears and trembling" they "began to pray to God to helpe us in this Deplorable condition." But to what God did they pray? According to Little Ephraim, he and Ancona asked Thomas Jones for religious instruction after they were released from prison. They had heard of Charles Wesley, the famed Methodist hymnodist, and asked specifically to be brought to him "that we may soon come to have some knowledge of God." Their interest in Christianity raises intriguing questions about their motivation. They could well have simulated this sudden piety to facilitate their return home, but features of Efik religion and culture made the Efik unusually receptive to other belief systems. The evidence strongly suggests that the Robin Johns' conversions were genuine and lasting, but also useful as they negotiated their way through the Anglo-Atlantic World.

The Robin Johns may have learned the basic tenets of the Christian faith from the slave traders with whom they interacted at Old Calabar, but seamen were a notoriously irreligious lot. John Newton, the slave trader turned cleric, described the effect of the slave trade on those Europeans engaged in it; "I know of no method of getting money, not even that of robbing for it upon the highway, which has so direct a tendency to efface the moral sense, to rob the heart of every gentle and humane disposition, and to harden it, like steel, against all impressions of sensibility."[1] Despite their adoption of many of the trappings of English culture, particularly those that facilitated commerce, there is no evidence that any of the Efik converted to Christianity before the arrival of Presbyterian missionaries in the nineteenth century.

Could the Robin Johns' interest in Christianity have been tied to their desire for freedom? Although both legal thought and popular opinion on the subject was complex and varied, there was certainly a widely held belief on the part of many Englishmen and enslaved Africans that while Christians could enslave infidels, they could not legally enslave other Christians. Sir Thomas Coke, England's most influential legal theorist, ruled that Christians could enslave infidels, but no basis for chattel slavery existed in English common law. In 1729, after considerable legal wrangling and confusion, the English Attorney-General and Solicitor-General issued formal opinions arguing that baptism did not change the status of a slave brought to Great Britain. American colonists had already taken matters into their own hands, and beginning with Maryland in 1664, slave-holding colonies passed their own laws clearly stating that baptism did not confer freedom on slaves. Such legislation continued to be enacted in British America as late as 1781, and as the historian David Brion Davis has pointed out, "the continuing insistence of such legislation revealed a deep-seated doubt" about the effects of baptism on the legal status of slaves.[2]

In Virginia, where the Robin Johns spent the longest time in slavery, the question of the compatibility of Christianity and enslavement was a thorny one. The historian Edmund Morgan has noted that "before the 1660s it seems to have been assumed that Christianity and slavery were incompatible." Morgan found early examples of Africans and Indians who sued for their freedom and won it on the basis of baptism, but the Virginia Assembly closed that loophole in 1667. Still, doubts persisted. The doctrine of Christian equality inherently challenged the racist underpinnings of the slave system, and enslaved converts often transferred doctrines of spiritual freedom and equality into the secular realm. Despite the 1667 law, slaves did not lose hope that conversion might break their bonds. One Anglican clergyman in Virginia reported to his superior in 1729 that some enslaved converts believed that "at some time or another Christianity will help them to their freedom." A year later the Anglican minister James Blair reported that one factor contributing to a rumored slave rebellion was that a number of black converts believed "that the king designed that all christians should be made free." That belief persisted in England, where "much of the impetus behind conversion of English slaves came from the blacks themselves who widely—but mistakenly—believed that baptism or marriage bestowed automatic freedom." The role that Christianity played in inspiring slave revolts in the eighteenth and nineteenth centuries provides clear evidence that the link between Christian faith and freedom remained deeply embedded in African American Christianity.[3]

The Robin Johns might well have been exposed to these beliefs, which were gaining wide currency in Virginia owing to the rapid spread of evangelicalism in the 1760s and 1770s. The New Light Baptist and Methodist faiths, for example, spread to the Tidewater in the 1770s and especially to port cities, including Portsmouth and Norfolk, where the Robin Johns would have traveled on their master's ship. Methodist revivals began in Virginia in the 1760s. Indeed, the coastal region and its primary ports formed one of the Methodists' first conferences—a conference was a network of churches—and was the base of support of black Methodism in Virginia. Ancona implied that his faith in Christianity began in Virginia. When he described his suffering at the hands of John Thompson he wrote, "I Hop[e] almight[y] great God he observe me from all great Danger so did."[4] The "great God" he called upon could have been Abasi, the high god of the Efik, though the fact that he wrote this passage to Charles Wesley strongly suggests that he referred to the Christian God.

Knowledge of Methodism in Virginia could explain why the Robin Johns asked to meet Charles Wesley. Another possibility is that Thomas Jones, himself a Methodist, directed them to the Wesleys, though the records suggest that the request originated with the Robin Johns themselves. The fact that they made their request only after they were freed from their jail cell is also suggestive. Had they sought to use conversion to build a case for their manumission, surely they would have adopted it while their case hung in the balance. It is possible that they saw conversion as additional "insurance" against any attempt to reenslave them before they reached Old Calabar, but it seems more likely that their conversions were genuine.

If Ancona and Little Ephraim found Jesus under the ministry of Charles and John Wesley, how can their attraction to Methodism be understood? Elements of Efik religion and culture can help to answer this question. The introduction of Ekpe and its ready adoption demonstrate that the Efik were open to other belief systems. Early missionaries found the Efik to be remarkably inclusive in their worship and reported that they quite easily shifted their attendance between Christian and traditional worship "without any pangs of conscience." Nineteenth-century missionaries in Old Calabar reported that the Efik believed that the powers of their god stopped at Parrot Island and that "the God of the white man" presided over the sea. Although it is impossible to read backward from such sources with any certainty, if the Robin Johns shared that view it could explain why they looked to the Christian god for assistance.[5]

Another factor in their conversion could be the Efik slave traders' eagerness to adopt aspects of English culture and to be recognized as "gentlemen." The Efik embraced English clothing, housing, goods, language and even table manners, but not English religion. It may be that the hardened English slave traders accorded the Efik the status of gentlemen without concern for their religious beliefs, and they certainly made no efforts to convert them to Christianity, but the Robin Johns would have found a different situation outside Old Calabar. The English considered the Africans' heathenism to be a principal failing, "a fundamental defect which set them distinctly apart."[6] The Robin Johns' conversion removed one of the most obvious marks of their otherness and opened the door to a world of close fellowship and support among the hardy Methodists of Bristol.

Methodism attracted African and African American converts in British North America and in England, and the Robin Johns' experience can be compared with that of other Africans in the eighteenth century. A number of enslaved Africans and African Americans who recorded their experiences during that period converted to Christianity. Almost all of them joined dissenting sects, and a surprising number converted to Methodism. John Marrant, Olaudah Equiano, and Robert Wedderburn, the authors of three important eighteenth-century slave narratives, all found salvation among the Methodists. Were there unique characteristics of Methodism that attracted them? Methodists reached out to humble folk, and their rituals and practices, including class meetings, love feasts, and extempore preaching and prayer, ushered converts into a supportive and emotional network of believers where each individual was considered precious in the sight of God. They rejected many of the traditional social values of the day, including those based on race, and offered all comers an ecstatic release from their sins and isolation. Ultimately, Methodists sought "a collective, emancipating sense of divine power."[7] It is no wonder that Africans and African Americans were drawn to them.

Conversion marked another step in the Robin Johns' ongoing process of creolization. Throughout the Americas, slaves found in Christianity a language of protest, liberation, and reform, and they appropriated it, melded it with traditional African beliefs, and created their own rich, synthetic religious systems. When Africans or African Americans experienced the evangelical New Birth, they found a sense of release and spiritual empowerment that one scholar referred to as "the liberated *self*—sanctified and redeemed." The Robin Johns prayed that "God will make we have strength and Knowledge to serve him." Strength and knowledge—those attributes had served the men well in their quest for freedom and their possession of them challenged the negative views of Africans' spiritual and cultural capacities held by many Englishmen. Edward Long, a contemporary of the Robin Johns, wrote a popular history of Jamaica in which he outlined the character of Africans as "brutish, ignorant, idle, crafty, treacherous, bloody, thievish, mistrustful, and superstitions people." His negative views were widely shared across the Anglo-Atlantic, but the Robin Johns certainly defied those stereotypes, and they used their faith as one means of winning acceptance and inspiring confidence. For example, when they made their depositions before their case came before Lord Mansfield, they proclaimed, "We, Little Ephraim Robin-John and Ancona Robin Robin John, believing in One God, the Creator of the world, and that God is a rewarder of them that do well, and an avenger of those that do ill; do swear."[8] Conversion, then, put the Robin Johns in a position to call for justice, to rebel against their enslavement, and to demand that their fellow Christians hear and believe them. In this sense, conversion was an act of defiance, an effort to erase concepts of difference and inferiority based on race through religion, the only belief system that militated against the prevailing racial ideology.

Bristol was the cradle of English Methodism; John Wesley first preached outdoors there and the first Methodist meetinghouse was built in the city. The Methodists drew large and emotional crowds; indeed, John Wesley claimed in 1739 that he could "advance the glory of God and the salvation of souls better in Bristol than anywhere else." While John Wesley traveled by horseback to carry his message across the British Isles, his brother, Charles, made his home in Bristol until his move to London in 1771. (There he renewed his friendship with Lord Mansfield, his childhood friend from Westminister School. There is no evidence that the two discussed the Robin Johns' case, but they may well have been in contact during that time). Though no longer a resident of Bristol, Charles and his family continued to make frequent visits there. Charles's wife, Sally, gave birth to eight children, but only three survived to adulthood, Charles (born 1757), Sally (born 1759), and Samuel (born 1766), and the entire family became friends of the Robin Johns. Best known as a writer of hymns, Charles was also a gifted preacher. Charles's wife left an affectionate description of her husband as "tender, indulgent, kind . . . warmly and unbelievably devoted to his friends, discerning in the character of men, incapable of disguise . . . As a preacher he was impassioned and energetic and expressed the most important truths with simplicity, brevity and force."[9]

Little Ephraim and Ancona began to study regularly with Charles Wesley, and Little Ephraim reported that they "felt Better and Better and to my comfort I Dreamt of reading two nights the last night I Dreamt I . . . read the 100 Psalm and . . . found good for my heart." A joyful song of praise, Psalm 100 hints at the universalist appeal of Christianity and the unity of all believers ("Make a joyful noise unto the Lord, all ye lands . . . we are his people, and the sheep of his pasture.") Little Ephraim's dreams of reading are one vivid indication of the importance of literacy to the Robin Johns, and their letters to Wesley demonstrate how quickly they advanced in their studies. Soon, "they received the truth with all gladness, appeared to be deeply penetrated therewith: and after some time, desired to be baptized." Through Charles, they also met John Wesley, and took every opportunity to meet with him and hear him preach. Perhaps they heard him preach from one of his favorite passages of Scripture from the Gospel of Luke: "The Spirit of the Lord is upon Me, because He hath anointed me to preach the gospel to the poor. He hath sent me to heal the broken-hearted; to preach deliverance to the captives, and . . . to set at liberty them that are bruised."[10]

In August 1774, Ancona wrote Charles, "yesterday we

had the pleasure of Seeing your brother he preached at the Room both morning and Evening & Drank Tea at Mrs. Johnson with us." They took communion from him on that occasion and "felt very comfortable in our mind." Charles called them "very extraordinary Scholars & Catechumens" and described their emotional baptism: "this morning I baptized them. They received both the outward and visible signs of the inward & spiritual grace in a wonderful manner & measure." Certainly Charles, who was "discerning in the character of men," had no doubt as to the sincerity of their conversions and held the Robin Johns in deep affection.[11]

The young men cut quite a figure in Bristol. Both were described as about five fee and nine inches in height, "well shaped, neither fat nor lean, and exactly proportioned." Their careful grooming as members of Old Calabar's elite showed; "they were perfectly well-bred; all their motions were easy, proper and graceful, notwithstanding their colour, there was something agreeable in their countenance." Despite their similarities, "there was a manifest difference both in their look and carriage. *Anacona* was all Sweetness; *Ephraim* was all a Prince. No one would have Conceived that he knew what slavery meant."[12]

The Robin Johns formed a close attachment to Charles and his family and to the Methodists in Bristol. They closed letters to Wesley with "kind love to Mrs. Wesley and too [two] young gentlemen." They even carried on a direct correspondence with his daughter, Sarah, whom they addressed as "My Dear Sarah." In one such letter, they "Received your Letter and am sorry you are angry with us for not writing to you when we did to your Brother but hopes you will for give us for it and hopes your prayer will all ways be for us . . . our Love to your father, Mother and Brother and all our Brethren," a letter they signed, "Your Loving Brethren." Such warm and personal greetings were a part of the conventional correspondence between the Old Calabar elite and their English traders, though the personal relationships reflected in this mutual correspondence go well beyond the merely formal. The Robin Johns lodged with Methodists, regularly took part in their meetings, and received individual instruction from pious Methodist women like Elizabeth Johnson.[13]

Elizabeth Johnson was a member of Wesley's innermost circle in Bristol, and he often lodged with her when he came to town. Her father, a West Indian merchant, opposed her conversion to Methodism and cut her out of his will entirely. Wesley regarded her as one of the most faithful women in the Methodist connection, and referred to her as "a *rara avis in terris*" (a bird rarely seen on earth). He praised her "great calmness and meekness," though he added that she wanted "more softness and tenderness . . . more of human mingled with the divine." But he found her cold and stoical and confessed that even after an acquaintance of over thirty years he could not feel real friendship and freedom with her. The Robin Johns, however, had a very different relationship with Miss Johnson, whose care and concern for the men reveals another side of her character.[14] Their association with her placed them at the center of Methodist life in Bristol, and the picture of the Robin Johns, John Wesley, and Elizabeth Johnson sitting down to converse over tea raises yet another series of questions.

What drew the Methodists to the Robin Johns, and no ordinary Methodists either, but the Wesleys themselves? Again, several alternative explanations present themselves. Were the Robin Johns exotic trophies, the ultimate symbols of the power of Methodism to convert the heathen? There are certainly hints of this attitude in some of the records surrounding the men and their complex relationship with the English Methodists. Stories of enslaved African princes became a literary trope in eighteenth-century British literature. In 1688 Aphra Behn published a novel entitled *Oroonoko; or the History of the Royal Slave*, the tragic story of an African slave-trading prince who was captured and sold into slavery in Surinam. Her story, adapted for the stage and widely translated, became one of the most popular stories of the eighteenth century and the source of the image of the noble African slave. In a rare case of life imitating art, in 1749 two African princes attended a performance of the play in London. They entered the theater to a standing ovation, and the audience looked on as one of the princes was so overcome by the performance that he fled the theater while the other watched in tears. There was not a dry eye in the house. In a tale similar to the Robin Johns', the princes had been sent to London to be educated, but had been kidnapped and sold in the Americas by a deceitful captain. By the 1770s and 1780s, many of England's most famous writers, including William Blake, Robert Burns, Samuel Taylor Coleridge, and William Wordsworth had taken up the plight of the noble African slave. Englishmen showed little sympathy for the millions of slaves sent to the New World or for the thousands of slaves and impoverished free blacks in England itself, but, as one scholar noted, "your free-born Briton could feel for a prince, particularly a prince in distress."[15]

But unlike almost all of their contemporaries in the English church or the literary world, John and Charles Wesley had seen American slavery firsthand when they traveled to the colony of Georgia as missionaries in 1736, and that experience left them with a sympathy for the enslaved that never wavered. With high hopes of converting the American Indians, John and Charles suffered an agonizing Atlantic crossing to take up their posts, John in Savannah and Charles in Frederica. The Wesleys scarcely laid eyes on natives, but they did encounter African slaves, and they were deeply shocked by what they saw. Slavery was prohibited in Georgia, but flourished in neighboring South Carolina, where slaves made up a majority of the population. On his visits there, John was deeply distressed by the slaveowners' complete lack of interest in the spiritual welfare of the men and women they held in bondage. He took every opportunity to talk with slaves and to minister to them. John Wesley's personal encounter with slavery made a profound impression on him, so overpowering that "in the last months of his American ministry, and in his vehement denunciation of chattel slavery thereafter, giving the gospel to slaves was a constant, recurrent goal he seemed scarcely able to get out of his mind." Charles had less direct contact with enslaved Africans than his brother, but nonetheless shared John's abhorrence of slavery. Charles filled his journal with descriptions of the horrid punishments inflicted on slaves and added, "It were endless to recount all the shocking instances of diabolical cruelty these men (as they [the slaveowners] call themselves) daily practice upon their fellow-creatures."[16]

Although the Wesleys' American experience lay over thirty years behind them when they encountered the Robin Johns, the horrors of slavery were burned into their minds, and the plight of enslaved and native Africans still concerned them. They would have encountered enslaved Africans and African Americans in the teaming slave port of Bristol, and the Robin Johns were not the first African converts to Methodism. In 1758, for example, John "baptized two negroes . . . one of these is deeply convinced of sin; the other rejoices in God her Saviour, and is the first African Christian I have known.

But shall not our Lord, in due time, have these Heathens also 'for his inheritance?'" Charles also made black converts. For example, he frequently took his ministry to the infamous Newgate Prison in London. Among his converts was "a poor black that had robbed his master," who found Jesus and became "quite happy." In one sermon, John asked,

> who cares for thousands, myriads, if not millions of the wretched Africans? Are not whole droves of these poor sheep (human, if not rational beings!) continually driven to market, and sold, like cattle, into the vilest bondage, without any hope of deliverance but by death? . . . O Father of mercies! are these the works of thy own hands, the purchase of thy Son's blood?

In 1772 John read "a very different book, published by an honest Quaker, on that execrable sum of all villanies, commonly called the Slave Trade." The pamphlet, by Anthony Benezet, a prominent Quaker from Philadelphia, confirmed Wesley's worst conceptions of the trade: "I read of nothing like it in the heathen world, whether ancient or modern: And it infinitely exceeds, in every instance of barbarity, whatever Christian slaves suffer in Mahometan countries." Benezet may well have sent Wesley his pamphlet as a part of his effort to enlist the support of English religious leaders, including the Archbishop of Canterbury, in the cause of abolition. The two men began a correspondence, and soon the story of the Robin Johns was crisscrossing the Atlantic as Wesley told Benezet about the plight of the Robin Johns and the massacre. Benezet recognized the potential value of the massacre for discrediting the trade and punishing the English captains who had participated in it. Immediately upon hearing of the Robin Johns and their story, Benezet dashed off a letter to his fellow abolitionist Granville Sharp in England in which he described the Robin Johns and the bloody event. He placed particular blame on Captain Bivins, and asked, "Now in this Case or any other of the like nature, which I believe frequently happen, would it not be right to endeavor to get the matter proved, & the Villian and his Accomplices, who have so flagrantly transgressed the Laws of God & Man, arraigned and brought to justice. It would, I am persuaded, be in several respects productive of good." Benezet enjoyed his greatest success with Wesley, and by 1772 he was referring to the founder of Methodism as "my friend John Westly." The following year Wesley met the Robin Johns, whose personal experiences gave vivid testimony of the evils of the slave trade.[17]

In 1774, shortly after John Wesley's close association with the Robin Johns came to a close, he published a landmark pamphlet in the crusade against the slave trade entitled *Thoughts upon Slavery*, which borrowed liberally from Benezet. Although Wesley made no direct mention of the Robin Johns, his conversations with them, perhaps those over Elizabeth Johnson's tea table, may well have shaped some of his thinking. He related the story of the Robin Johns to Benezet in a 1774 letter, which indicates that the princes were still in his thoughts as he wrote and published his pamphlet. He attacked the idea that Africa was "so remarkably horrid, dreary, and barren, that it is a kindness to deliver them [enslaved Africans] out of it." He described a fertile and rich land "some governed by kings, others by the principal men, who take care each of their own town or village" (an apt description of Old Calabar). As for religion, the Africans "believe there is one God, the Author of them and all things." He attacked the image of Africans perpetuated by writers like Edward Long. He argued that Africans were not "senseless, brutish, lazy barbarians," but rather "remarkably sensible . . . industrious to the highest degree . . . mild, friendly, and kind to strangers." He concluded that "certainly the African is in no respect inferior to the European." David Brion Davis observed that in Wesley's view, Africans "behaved like potential Methodists." Given his conversion of the Robin Johns, he had every reason to believe that Africans *were* potential converts, a belief he would act on in later years.[18]

One reason that the slave trade weighed so heavily on John Wesley's mind in 1774 may well have been his efforts to convince the Robin Johns of its evils. Wesley roundly condemned slave traders as "man-stealers," a phrase that he employed frequently. In his 1743 *Explanatory Notes upon the New Testament* he wrote, "*Man-stealers*—The worst of all thieves, in comparison of whom Highwaymen and House-breakers are innocent!" We can only wonder if he spoke so bluntly to the Robin Johns, the first *African* slave traders he had confronted; certainly he was not a man to pull a spiritual punch, and the Robin Johns hint that he made his feelings known. In August 1773 Little Ephraim informed Charles Wesley that "Your Brother has been so kind as to talk to us and has given us the Sacrament thrice[.] I find him so good as he shew me when I do wrong[.] I feel in my heart great trouble & see great deal more of my own faults & the faults of my Countrymen which I hope the Lord will permit me to tell them when I com home." Though Little Ephraim does not specifically say so, Wesley very likely condemned the Efik's involvement in the slave trade as the principal fault of his countrymen. While he condemned the Africans who participated in the trade, his remarks to the Robin Johns may have been tempered by his belief that the ultimate responsibility for the trade rested squarely on the shoulders of the European slave traders and planters. It was the European slavers who enticed Africans into preying on one another; it was they who introduced alcohol and firearms and helped foment the wars that produced slave captives.[19]

Encouraged by the Wesleys and nurtured by the close Methodist fellowship in Bristol, the Robin Johns converted to Christianity and were baptized, took every opportunity to attend preaching and other religious meetings, and pored over Scripture. Their heartfelt conversions mark yet another step in their acculturation after over six years spent in the Americas and England. Encouraged by aspects of Efik religion and culture, including a receptivity to English culture, by the nature of evangelicalism, and by the Wesleys' personal interest in the plight of slaves, the Robin Johns found a faith that sustained them through their trials and tribulations and enabled them to challenge their captors and win their freedom. In a letter to Charles Wesley, Ancona probably spoke for Little Ephraim as well when he gave thanks to the "almight[y] great God" who had protected him "from all great Danger" and "gave me knowledge to remember what I have suffered."[20]

6

"We Go Home to Old Calabar"

The Robins Johns' Legacy in
Old Calabar and England

*A*fter several months in Bristol, the Robin Johns hoped that their long-sought voyage home was about to begin; in mid-August they wrote Charles Wesley that "our good friend Mr. Jones is fitted a ship out for us[;] we suppose she will be ready in about five weeks." He also reported that he had heard from his brother, Grandy King George, via a captain recently back from Old Calabar who had passed on the good news that Little Ephraim and Ancona were alive and on their way home. By February 1774 the vessel Jones had outfitted, the *Maria,* was ready to leave and set sail, but it was forced to come back in again, "the Wind being Contrary for We go home to Old Calabar." Six days later the ship still remained in port, and Little Ephraim and Ancona wrote

Charles to thank him for his gift of religious books. They expressed their gratitude to Charles and his family for their prayers that they would arrive safely "in our Deserved Country." They sent love to the entire Wesley family, and wished for a "Knowledge of God Equall to your self." They signed themselves, "your poor and Loving Brethren Till Death." On March 12, 1774, the *Maria* set sail. The ship had not been fitted out especially for the Robin Johns. It was a slave ship, the veteran of several voyages, and on its previous voyages had taken on 525 slaves in Africa, 437 of whom had been delivered to the Caribbean. William Floyd was the ship's captain. In yet another twist to the story, Floyd had been present at the massacre where the Robin Johns were captured, serving as second captain on board the *Indian Queen*, and had given the crucial deposition in the Robin Johns' case before Lord Mansfield.[1]

With high hopes, Little Ephraim and Ancona set out for home, only to face further trials. The *Maria* wrecked off a desert island called Boa Vista, an accident that Ephraim and Ancona blamed on the drunken incompetence of Captain Floyd. Apparently, "the vessel was dashed to pieces against ye rocks & sunk & all ye crew escaped only with theyr lives in a small Boat after which they were near starved." Rescued by a passing ship, the Africans returned to Bristol "drest in borrow'd rags." They ran to Charles's house, but he was away, and they hurried to the home of Elizabeth Johnson. Even though "all was disappointment," she took them in and found them "greatly distressed but yet confident," and "above all," she reported that they "are at a loss to know ye voice of God." Their Methodists friends rallied around them; as Miss Johnson put it, "our pain for them is not to be described."[2]

Despite their outward confidence, the enormous setback affected the men, especially Ephraim. Elizabeth Johnson found them to be "very gratefull [and] desirous of doing every thing they can to oblige they are as assidious as they can be both to read & understand, it is an arduous task for them to take in ye sense, but I Bless God I see He does assist them." She noted, however, that "Ephraim is greatly altered[,] more thoughtful & humble. He often speaks of feeling in his Heart . . . I frequently see great heavings of heart upon Ephraim[.] I believe he sees & fears approaching difficulties. Seems so full for Mr. Jones's expenses." Ancona, by contrast, "is as easy as a Bird without care or fear." Miss Johnson reported that they spent their time studying Scripture and attending services, where "some of our preachers felt great union with them[,] talked with them & prayed for them." She added, "it seems as if they are appointed for usefulness[;] you would be pleased to hear how they see the idleness & stupidity of theyre past lives," probably another reference to their involvement in the slave trade. They also humored their hosts by attempting to learn skills that the English believed would be useful at home;

for instance, they studied gardening and agriculture, and learned to make butter and cheese.[3]

Thomas Jones posed one problem. Apparently his kindness had been exhausted or, more likely, the Africans were proving more of an economic liability than an asset. He complained of the large sums he had spent on their upkeep, and refused to have anything more to do with them. Miss Johnson told Charles Wesley that the Robin Johns had given Charles as much information as they could about their circumstance, but she believed that "much has been concealed . . . [the] barbarity by poor Mr. Jones . . . has increased much[.] He will . . . seem to *have pleasure in ye wreck of ye Ship.*" Little Ephraim, however, refused to see that duplicity and, like a trader-prince and Ekpe member, worried about paying the debt he had accumulated. He asked Charles Wesley, "One Question I have to aske you before we Leave England which is most on my Mind that this how shall I pay My good friend Mr. Jones who has been so kind in Laying out so much money to save us[?]" Ephraim could see only one way to repay Jones—a chilling one considering his own experience. He wrote, "if we must not sell slaves I know not how we shall pay[,] which I have a great desire to doe."[4]

That the Robin Johns considered reentering the slave trade after their own experience with its horrors may be shocking to modern sensibilities, but the princes operated within an African system of ethics that their conversion to Christianity could not entirely erase. They returned to a society in which slavery and the slave trade were deeply embedded; indeed, there was little opposition to "the trade in principle, on the part either of African societies collectively or of their ruling elites." Nor was their view exceptional in the wider Atlantic World. Opponents to slavery and the slave trade were still a tiny minority in Europe, and were scarcely heard at all in the slave-holding societies of the Americas. African societies recognized slavery as an institution governed by a set of rules; "they felt strongly that there were legal limits to who could be enslaved and when." As the Robin Johns argued before Lord Mansfield, they had been illegally enslaved by the laws of their own country. They did not suggest that enslavement itself was illegal, only that their own enslavement had been in violation of Efik law and custom. Their case "reflected the existence of a class, as well as a racial, dimension to the operation of the slave trade," distinctions that Africans and European slave traders understood very well. Indeed, the efforts of slave traders such as Thomas Jones to liberate members of the African slave-trading elite who had been wrongfully enslaved actually served to legitimate the enslavement of other Africans and reinforced their own reputation for fair dealing. African elites sought to establish "a proper order of enslavement and an orderly slave trade," one that was conducted by African rules, not governed by the greed and arrogance of European traders. As the long conduct of the trade suggests, African and European slave traders had arrived at mutually understood rules about who should be enslaved, though individuals on both sides sometimes violated those rules. Still, "it seems clear that African thinking on the slave trade closely paralleled that of contemporary (pre-abolitionist) Europe." If the Robin Johns chose to ignore Wesley's views on the subject, it is no more than many white Methodists did, and was in keeping with the selective creolization process in which Africans incorporated the aspects of European culture that best suited their own needs.[5]

By September 1774, a reluctant Jones, still bound by the agreement before Mansfield's court, had arranged another passage, and the Robin Johns prepared to depart. Their letters to Charles Wesley were even more affectionate than previously. Casting aside the more formal salutations that had characterized their correspondence ("Revd Sir," or "Reverend father in God," for example), they addressed the final letters before their departure to "My Dear Charles." Little Ephraim promised "never to forget" his friend, and added "our kindest love a waits your sister & Brother[,] accept the same for yourself." He added "P[.]S.[.] I Desire your sister to write to me." Ancona's affectionate nature shines though in his heartfelt farewell to Charles, "I fear this will be the last I shall be able to write to you . . . you have bin so good to us that we can never thank you enough for your love to us but now we must take our Leave with Litting [letting] you know how kind our Bristol friends have been to us." Even John Wesley came to say his farewells and give them his blessing. Ancona continued, "we had a very Blessed time last night with Mr. Wesley who offered us up in a very solemn manner to God and we Humbly hope his prayer will be heard[.] I must conclude with kindest love to all." Ephraim could not resist adding one last note to his brother's letter, "I hope . . . we shall hear from one another again[.] I now bid you farewell Dear Charles." On October 14, 1774, Ephraim and Ancona sailed for Old Calabar on board the *Cato,* a slave ship owned by Jones.[6]

Their Bristol friends worried as the brothers embarked on their journey, and the Methodists in Bristol missed their exceptional brothers in Christ; as one of them wrote to Charles, "We remember them at ye Room (the New Room in Bristol where Methodist services were held) & doubt not but you do still more at London." Over a year passed before the good news arrived; Charles wrote happily that "my 2 African Children got safe home." Ancona wrote back that they were welcomed at Old Calabar, but their newfound religious views caused some problems initially; "many of their countrymen . . . [who] wondered and laughed at first, were now glad to sit by and hear them read the Bible." No doubt they read from one of the Bibles Charles sent with them. Evidence suggests that Little Ephraim did engage in the slave trade after his return; he had little choice, as he suggested to Wesley, given the economic importance of the trade to Old Calabar and his position in the family. Oral tradition from Old Calabar relates that Little Ephraim and Ancona were responsible for the spread of Christianity there after their return. One Calabar historian wrote, "It is a well-known fact among the Efiks of Old Calabar that . . . two Efik graduates of Ambo Otu [also Mbo Otu or King Robin] descent from Obutong [Old Town] were carried away in the 1767 'bombardment.' It was they who came in the nineteenth century back to Calabar to lead the Old Calabar 'nobles' to demand the coming of the Presbyterian Mission."[7]

But is this oral tradition reliable? Did the Robin Johns invite the first Presbyterian missionaries to Old Calabar? The chronology raises serious doubts. The Presbyterian missionaries arrived in Old Calabar in 1846, far too late for the Robin Johns to have been involved. A closer examination of the record reveals that the oral history was not completely wrong, though different events had become somewhat conflated over time. The minutes of the 1778 Methodist Conference record a discussion about the establishment of an African mission in Old Calabar, a discussion that lasted several hours and "was marked by deep piety, sound sense, and powerful eloquence." The proposal to send Methodist missionaries to Africa originated with Little Ephraim and Ancona, who apparently remained in contact with their Methodist friends and "desired that Missionaries might be sent to instruct them [the Efik] in the English language, and the great principles of Christianity." Their "faithful friend" Elizabeth Johnson had died since their departure, but she remembered the Robin Johns and left a legacy of £500 to support a mission to Old Calabar. The Conference approved the mission and appointed two missionaries, brothers named Syndrum who were natives of Germany but members of the Methodist Society at Bristol. They arrived in Old Calabar, and "were treated by the uncle of the princes with all possible attention." Despite the promising beginning, the Syndrum brothers quickly succumbed to the dangerous diseases of West Africa, long a graveyard for Europeans who lacked immunities to tropical diseases. When news of their deaths reached England, Dr. Thomas Coke sent a circular to all young Methodist itinerant preachers asking for volunteers to continue the work. At least one volunteer came forward, but John Wesley refused to accept him, and the mission was abandoned.[8]

So the oral history from Old Calabar was not entirely wrong; the Robin Johns were responsible for bringing the first Christian missionaries to Old Calabar, but in 1778 not in 1846. It may be that their efforts to bring missionaries left a lasting impression among their countrymen and if so that may help explain why the rulers of Duke Town and Creek Town invited missionaries to return to Old Calabar in the 1840s. In 1843 British officials undertook negotiations in Old Calabar for a treaty to abolish the slave trade there. Eyo Honesty II of Creek Town, King Eyamba of Duke Town, and Willy Tom Robins of Old Town sought missionaries primarily as teachers, just as the Robin Johns "desired that Missionaries might be sent to instruct them in the English language." Eyo Honesty, the chief advocate for opening a mission in Old Calabar, became king of Creek Town in 1825 and could well have known the Robin Johns. He, too, spoke and read English and served as a cabin boy on an English vessel in his youth. It does not appear that the Robin Johns' efforts to teach Christianity made any lasting impression in Old Calabar; at least the early missionaries found no trace of Christian worship there.[9]

As their correspondence with the Methodists indicates, the Robin Johns were not completely forgotten in England. English Methodists held them up as examples of heathens who had converted and serialized their story in the *Arminian Magazine* in 1783. Other writers used their story as an example of "the excellency of our laws, which do not tolerate slavery in any part of the United Kingdom." Although the Robin Johns did not speak out against the slave trade in England as Equiano did, their story was employed by opponents of slavery including Wesley, Anthony Benezet, and Thomas Clarkson. In 1787, a group of Quaker abolitionists, joined by a handful of other reformers including Granville Sharp and Thomas Clarkson, organized an antislavery society. The group was opposed to both slavery and the slave trade, but ultimately agreed that taking on both of these "evils" at once was likely to fail. After considerable debate, they agreed that "by aiming at the abolition of the Slave-trade they were laying the axe at the very root," and they called themselves the Society for Effecting the Abolition of the Slave Trade. Clarkson, whom Samuel Taylor Coleridge described as "the moral steam engine" of the movement, set out to collect evidence for the Society's campaign and began to organize local societies. Clarkson headed for Bristol, and as he approached the city on horseback, he began to doubt the wisdom of attacking a commerce that was so vital to the city's prosperity, but concluded that "no labor should make me shrink, nor danger, nor even persecution, [should] deter me from my pursuit."[10]

As Clarkson sought evidence of the evils of the slave trade, he began to hear rumors of the Massacre of 1767 and the capture and enslavement of the Robin Johns. Like Benezet, he recognized that the massacre was just the sort of event the opponents of the trade needed. He wrote that even though "this cruel transaction had been frequently mentioned to me . . . as it had taken place twenty years before, I could not find one person who had been engaged in it, nor could I come, in a satisfactory manner, at the various particulars belonging to it." His luck changed when he met Henry Sulgar, a Moravian minister in Bristol, who provided him with "authentic documents relative to the treacherous massacre at Calabar." Through Sulgar, Clarkson obtained the depositions from *The King v. Lippincott,* the 1773 court case involving the Robin Johns. Clarkson was shocked by what he read:

> The knowledge of this tragical event [the Massacre of 1767] now fully confirmed me in the sentiment, that the hearts of those, who were concerned in this traffic, became unusually hardened, and that I might readily believe any atrocities, however great, which might be related of them. It made also my blood boil as it were within me. It gave a new spring to my exertions. And I rejoiced, sorrowful as I otherwise was, that I had visited Bristol, if it had been only to gain an accurate statement of this one fact.[11]

Like Benezet before him, Clarkson recognized that the bloodbath could provide damning evidence against the trade and arouse public sympathy.

After gathering a good deal of damning information on the trade at Bristol, Clarkson traveled to Liverpool, where Captain Thomas Chaffers introduced him to Captain Ambrose Lace over breakfast. Clarkson did not connect Lace with the Massacre of 1767 until the captain mentioned Old Calabar; then, Clarkson wrote,

> a kind of horror came over me. His name became directly associated in my mind with the place. It al-

most instantly occurred to me that he commanded
the Edgar out of Liverpool, when the dreadful
massacre . . . took place. Indeed I seemed to be so
confident of it, that, attending more to my feelings
than to my reason at this moment, I accused him
with being concerned in it. This produced great
confusion among us. For he looked incensed at captain Chaffers, as if he had introduced me to him for
this purpose. Captain Chaffers again seemed to be
all astonishment that I should have known of this
circumstance, and to be vexed that I should have
mentioned it in such a manner. I was also in a state
of trembling myself. Captain Lace could only say it
was a bad business. But he never defended himself,
nor those concerned in it. And we soon parted, to
the great joy of us all.[12]

The Society for Effecting the Abolition of the Slave
Trade had not been idle in Clarkson's absence. Committee members began to solicit support from friends across
the country and in America. Support came from prominent individuals such as John Wesley, who offered to
publish and distribute a new, enlarged edition of his
Thoughts upon Slavery with favorable mention of the Society and its work, and Josiah Wedgwood, who joined
the committee. More important, perhaps, the Society
quickly gained support from cities, towns, churches, ves-
tries, and other civic organizations. All sorts of public

and private meeting places were opened to the Society, and it launched a remarkably successful petition drive. The Society's press was kept busy virtually around the clock as thousands of circulars and antislavery pamphlets rolled off it. Petitions condemning the trade began to pour into Parliament, and in 1788 Parliament began an investigation into the conduct of the trade. The Society for Effecting the Abolition of the Slave Trade appointed Clarkson to gather evidence to be presented to the parliamentary committee.[13]

Both the slave-trade faction and the abolitionists felt confident of victory, and both groups "began a long game of calculating the most favorable time to stop examining or cross-examining witnesses." Clarkson had collected massive documentary evidence about the evils of the trade, but the parliamentary committee planned to hear from witnesses. Most of Clarkson's informants were sailors whose rough manners and lack of education made them poor candidates to appear before the gentlemen in Parliament. Many people who sympathized with the movement questioned Clarkson's tactics, including Wesley, who warned that "to *hire* or *pay* informers has a bad sound and might raise . . . insurmountable prejudice against you." In addition, many of his witnesses still depended on the trade for their livelihood, and he "found it difficult to prevail upon persons to be publicly examined on this subject."[14] Proponents of the trade had no such problems; they could call on prominent merchants, West

Indian planters (members of both groups sat in Parliament), and others who moved in high circles.

As a result, the investigation did not go very well for the abolitionists, and Clarkson knew that if a vote were to be taken, the supporters of the trade would be victorious. He set out on another trip to try to persuade more men to testify, but despite growing public opposition to the trade, he could not persuade most of his informants to testify in public. He traveled sixteen hundred miles and took information from forty-seven people, only nine of whom agreed to testify. In the meantime, however, prominent witness after witness testified to the importance of the trade for British commerce and the health of the empire, to the benefits of the trade to the Africans themselves (including the benefits of Christianity), and to the dangers that abolitionist agitation posed in stirring up rebellion in the sugar islands. Parliamentary maneuvering delayed the hearings. Discouraged but undaunted, Clarkson set out once again to find informants willing to testify. He searched particularly for men with firsthand knowledge of the conduct of the trade in Africa. He traveled from port to port, and even boarded over 160 warships in search of sailors with such information. Finally, on board one of those warships, he found George Millar, "a very respectable person," who had been on board the *Canterbury* during the Massacre of 1767. Millar was willing to testify! In addition, he found Isaac Parker, the sailor who had lived in Old Calabar for several months, one of the few Englishmen who had actually taken part in a slave-raiding expedition with African slave traders. Parker, too, was willing to take the stand.[15]

With these successes, Clarkson "returned now in triumph." His important new witnesses, when added to those who had already agreed to appear, made the opponents of the trade "more formidable than at any former period; so that the delay of our opponents, which we had looked upon as so great an evil, proved in the end truly serviceable to us." One after one, Clarkson's witnesses appeared before the committee, and their graphic and moving testimony had a major impact on the parliamentary investigation and on public opinion. Descriptions of the massacre played an important role in the hearings by focusing attention on the atrocities of the trade and on the violence and duplicity of the English slave traders. Clarkson's witnesses provided vivid and gruesome images that openly shocked the members of the House of Commons. Even the humble origins of most of Clarkson's witnesses ultimately proved to be an advantage, though, as Wesley had expected, opponents of abolition questioned Clarkson's witnesses about their low salaries and about any subsidies or payments they had received from the antislavery advocates. Supporters of the trade claimed to have "produced persons in elevated life and of the highest character as witnesses," while opponents of the trade "had been obliged to take up with those of

the lowest condition." By 1792 the parliamentary debates
had exposed the horrors of the trade to the English people, who were further moved by abolitionist literature,
by the conversion of more and more clergymen, aristo-
crats, and other notables to the cause, and by a successful
boycott of rum and sugar to oppose the traffic in human
flesh. Even fashion played a part; Josiah Wedgwood
turned out thousands of cameos bearing the seal of the
Society, a black man in chains on his knees with the
motto "Am I Not a Man And A Brother." They appeared inlaid on gold snuffboxes, on women's bracelets,
or on pins in women's elaborate hairstyles. As Clarkson
put it, soon "the taste for wearing them became general;
and thus fashion, which usually confines itself to worth-
less things, was seen for once in the honourable office of
promoting the cause of justice, humanity, and freedom."
By 1794 the indefatigable Clarkson had made seven trips
across Britain in search of information and logged 35,000
miles. Despite swelling opposition to the African slave
trade, Parliament was reluctant to abolish it outright
since such a move might open the door to other even
more radical reform measures and could encourage slave
uprisings in the sugar islands (a slave rebellion on Dominica added to these fears). The result was a compromise
in which the House of Commons passed a resolution on
April 3, 1792, calling for the gradual abolition of the
trade. In 1805 Parliament went further and made it illegal
for British ships to supply slaves to any foreign market or

to any captured territory, an act that cut off more than half of the total British trade. Parliament finally abolished the trade in 1807.[16]

Even in Bristol, once the primary slave-trading port in England, the slave trade fell increasingly into disfavor, in large part because of the strength of dissenting sects such as the Methodists and Quakers. In 1791 a former mayor of the city informed William Wilberforce, the abolitionists' chief parliamentary spokesman, that "the slave trade is growing disgraceful," and the first anti-slave trade committee outside London was convened in Bristol. Prominent antislavery spokesmen, including Coleridge and Wesley, attracted large audiences there. When in 1788 Wesley prepared to deliver a stinging antislavery sermon at the New Room (where the Robin Johns had worshiped with their Methodist brethren), he announced his topic in advance to attract the largest possible congregation. The room was filled "from end to end" with "high and low, rich and poor." None was disappointed, for the occasion was one of the most exciting in Wesley's long career. As Wesley reported:

About the middle of the discourse, while there was on every side attention still as night, a vehement noise arose, none could tell why, and shot like lightening through the whole congregation. The terror and confusion were inexpressible. You might have imagined it was a city taken by storm. The people rushed upon each other with the utmost violence; the benches were broken in pieces, and nine-tenths of the congregation appeared to be struck with the same panic . . . In about six minutes the storm ceased . . . and all being calm, I went on without the least interruption. . . . It was the strangest incident of the kind I ever remember . . . Satan fought, lest his kingdom should be delivered up.

He followed that meeting with a day of fasting and prayer and asked God to "make a way for them [slaves] to escape, and break their chains in sunder." The proponents of the slave trade in the city were not completely overcome. When the House of Commons rejected Wilberforce's motion for a bill to abolish the slave trade in 1791, church bells pealed (Church of England bells, no doubt), bonfires and fireworks lit the skies, and sailors and workers were given a half-day holiday. Still, by the 1790s it must have appeared that antislavery had taken the city by storm, a change that would have seemed almost impossible when the Robin Johns first stepped ashore there twenty years earlier.[17]

Wesley did not live to see the abolition of the trade he so despised, though he went to his grave with the matter on his mind. The last letter he wrote was to Wilberforce, calling on his old ally to continue to fight the good fight; "Go on," Wesley urged, "in the name of God and in the power of His might, till even American slavery (the vilest that ever saw the sun) shall vanish away before it." At eighty-seven, Wesley was growing feeble. He spent his final days reading "a tract wrote by a poor African," Equiano's narrative. He died on March 2, 1791, and according to Wilberforce his dying words were "Slave Trade."[18]

The parliamentary committee was certainly correct when it described the Massacre of 1767 as a "remarkable transaction."[19] Forty years after the event, the massacre and the capture and enslavement of the Robin Johns continued to reverberate in Britain. Little Ephraim Robin John and Ancona Robin Robin John had their roles to play in the British abolition movement and in the first attempts to introduce Christianity to Old Calabar, but they may be most important as an illustration of the complex and remarkable history of the eighteenth-century Atlantic World. As Paul Gilroy wrote, the Atlantic was "continually crisscrossed by the movements of black people—not only as commodities but engaged in various struggles towards emancipation, autonomy, and citizenship." The princely Little Ephraim and free-spirited Ancona help counter the tendency to reduce Africans who suffered the horrors of the slave trade to commodities and numbers. Albert Camus in *The Plague* wrote that prisoners and exiles experience the profound suffering of living with memories that have no purpose. Prisoners and exiles they may have been, but the Robin Johns refused to give up their memories of home and their relationship with each other. Clearly, for these men, memory had a purpose. Memory nurtured them through the harsh realities of slavery in the Americas and kept alive their determination to return home. Their experience cannot be fully understood without recognizing the distinctive culture from which they came, a reminder of the importance of ethnic diversity among enslaved Africans. Old Calabar's strong economic, linguistic, and cultural ties to Britain, its creolized merchant elite and their unusual level of literacy and their understanding of trade, gave the Robin Johns a set of skills that most enslaved Africans lacked. Most, but not all, for their experience can be compared to that of creolized Luso-Africans, for example, and to the other Atlantic creoles whose stories are only beginning to be told. The Robin Johns were cosmopolitan products of the Atlantic World, and they became a part of the three worlds that composed it—Africa, the Americas, and Europe. Despite their years away from home and their deeper engagement with English culture, the Robin Johns remained Efik; and more than that, they remained Efik slave traders. They moved through the eighteenth-century Atlantic World in ways that would have been unthinkable for enslaved Africans without their knowledge and understanding. They were determined to return home and to their elite positions in the slave-trading society of Old Calabar. The Robin Johns made the most of their skills and accomplished what very few Africans did in the eighteenth century— escaped slavery, freed themselves, and returned to their "Deserved Country."[20]

Notes

Prologue

1. For examples of this scholarship see Alfred W. Crosby, *The Columbian Exchange: Biological and Cultural Consequences of 1492* (New York, 1973); Alison Games, *Migration and the Origins of the English Atlantic World* (Cambridge, Mass., 1999); D. W. Meinig, *The Shaping of America: A Geographical Perspective on 500 Years of History*, vol. 1: *Atlantic America, 1492–1800* (New Haven, 1986); Bernard Bailyn, *The Peopling of British North America: An Introduction* (New York, 1986); Jack P. Greene, *Pursuits of Happiness: The Social Development of Early Modern British Colonies and the Formation of American Culture* (Chapel Hill, 1988).

2. On Atlantic creoles see Ira Berlin, "From Creole to African: Atlantic Creoles and the Origins of African-American Society in Mainland North America," *William and Mary Quarterly*, 3rd ser., 53 (1996), quotation on p. 254.

3. Few topics in the study of the slave trade have provoked more debate than the numbers of slaves transported from Africa. The debate began with Philip D. Curtin's *The Atlantic Slave*

Trade: A Census (Madison, Wis., 1969). For a brief summary of the debate and the most current estimates see David Eltis, "The Volume and Structure of the Transatlantic Slave Trade: A Reassessment," *William and Mary Quarterly,* 3rd ser., 58 (Jan. 2001), 17–46.

4. Vincent Carretta, "Olaudah Equiano or Gustavus Vassa? New Light on an Eighteenth-Century Question of Identity," *Slavery and Abolition,* 20 (Dec. 1999), 96–105; S. E. Ogude, "Facts into Fiction: Equiano's Narrative Reconsidered," *Research in African Literatures,* 13 (Spring 1982), 31–43.

1. "A Very Bloody Transaction"

1. A letter from Grandy King George to Ambrose Lace, a slave trader from Bristol, provides an example of the rich array of luxury goods the slave traders of Old Calabar purchased with their profits. The details of the king's dress have been derived from this letter and from descriptions of the ceremonial canoes and costumes of later Old Calabar rulers. See Grandy King George to Ambrose Lace (undated), reproduced in Gomer Williams, *History of the Liverpool Privateers and Letters of Marque with an Account of the Liverpool Slave Trade* (New York, 1966), 545–546.

2. On literacy among the Old Calabar elite, see Paul E. Lovejoy and David Richardson, eds., "Letters of the Old Calabar Slave Trade, 1760–1789," in Vincent Caretta, ed., *Genius in Bondage: Literature of the Early Black Atlantic* (Louisville, 2001), 89–115.

3. John Ashley Hall's testimony in Shelia Lambert, ed., *House of Commons Sessional Papers of the Eighteenth Century,* vol. 72, "George III, Minutes of Evidence in the Slave Trade, 1790," Part 2 (Washington, D.C., 1975), 537.

4. The principal towns were close to one another, but distinct. Creek Town, built on the edge of a creek that links the Cross and Calabar rivers, was about twelve miles from Duke Town. Old Town was some three and a half miles above Duke Town. There is disagreement over the dates of the founding of the towns. For example, Ekei Essien Oku and Efiong U. Aye, Old Calabar historians, give the date for the founding of Duke Town as ca. 1650 and note that Creek Town, Duke Town, and New Town appear in John Barbot's journal (Barbot, a French resident of England working for the French Royal African Company, made voyages to Africa in 1678 and 1682). The historian David Northrup accepts this seventeenth-century date. See Northrup, *Trade without Rulers: Pre-Colonial Economic Development in South-Eastern Nigeria* (Oxford, 1978), 38. The historians Paul Lovejoy and David Richardson believe that Duke Town was not founded until the eighteenth century, while Eyo Okon Akak proposes even earlier dates than any of the others. See Ekei Essien Oku, *The Kings and Chiefs of Old Calabar (1785–1925)* (Calabar, Nigeria, 1989), 13–14, 25, and Efiong U. Aye, *Old Calabar through the Centuries* (Calabar, Nigeria, 1967), 2–3, 31–41. Lovejoy and Richardson, "Trust, Pawnship, and Atlantic History: The Institutional Foundations of the Old Calabar Slave Trade," *American Historical Review*, 104 (1999), 337, 340–341; Eyo Okon Akak, *Efiks of Old Calabar*, vol. 1: *Origin and History* (Calabar, Nigeria, 1982), 45–46; John Barbot, "A Description of the Coasts of North and South Guinea," in Thomas Astley and John Churchill, eds., *Collection of Voyages and Travels* (London, 1732). See also Monday Efiong Noah, *Old Calabar: The City States and the Europeans, 1800–1885* (Calabar, Nigeria, 1980), 2–18, 48–66; D. Simmons, "An Ethnographic Sketch of the Efik People," in Daryll Forde, ed., *Efik Traders of Old Calabar* (London, 1956), 3–4.

5. Hall's testimony, 557.

6. Northrup, *Trade without Rulers*, 88. Lovejoy and Richardson, "Trust, Pawnship, and Atlantic History," 340–341; Oku, *The Kings and Chiefs of Old Calabar*, 192–196; Nwanna Nzewunwa, "Pre-colonial Nigeria: East of the Niger," in Richard Olaniyan, ed., *Nigerian History and Culture* (Essex, Eng., 1985), 30–31.

7. Williams, *History of the Liverpool Privateers*, 533–535, 534–535. Berry made sixteen recorded voyages to the Bight of Biafra and brought over 4,300 slaves on board his ships. On this voyage he sailed on the *Dalrymple*. See David Eltis, Stephen D. Behrendt, David Richardson, and Herbert D. Klein, et al., eds., *Trans-Atlantic Slave Trade: A Database on CD-ROM* (Cambridge, Eng., 1999), Analysis, Summary (Any CAPTAIN = Berry). The term "palaver" is derived from the Portugese "palavra" meaning word and was used in Old Calabar's trade language to describe a discussion, debate, or conference. As this letter suggests, English captains adopted it as well.

8. James Morley's testimony in Lambert, ed., *House of Commons Sessional Papers*, vol. 73, 163. Morley reported that this event occurred in 1763 or 1764, when he was on board the *Amelia*. Captain James Briggs was there in 1764 on the *Sandwich*. See Eltis et al., eds., *Trans-Atlantic Slave Trade*, Unique Identity Numbers 17538 and 91062. Parker's testimony, 133.

9. Williams, *History of the Liverpool Privateers*, 535.

10. The details of the massacre have been reconstructed from the following sources: George Millar's testimony in Lambert, ed., *House of Commons Sessional Papers*, vol. 73, 385–387; Captain John Ashley Hall's testimony in Lambert, ed., *House of Commons Sessional Papers*, vol. 72, 515–517, 528–529, 537–538, 556–557, 559; Captain Ambrose Lace's testimony, in Lambert, ed., *House of Commons Sessional Papers*, vol. 72, 633–636; Thomas Clarkson, *The History of the Rise, Progress, and Accomplishment of the Abolition of the African Slave-Trade by the British Parliament*, 2

vols. (1808; rpt. London, 1968), vol. 1, 305–310; Ancona Robin John to Charles Wesley, Aug. 17, 1774, in Charles Wesley Papers, John Rylands Library, Manchester, Eng.; *Arminian Magazine*, 6 (Feb. 1783), 98–99; ibid., (March 1783), 151; Public Record Office (henceforth PRO), KB 1/19/3, Mich. 1773, affidavit of William Floyd, Sept. 30, 1773. Ancona Robin Robin John and Little Ephraim Robin John were able to give the names of either the ships or their captains and ports of origin in 1774. Using their information and the *Trans-Atlantic Slave Trade Database*, one can identify all the ships and captains and confirm their presence in Old Calabar in 1767 (see Unique Identity Numbers 17671, 17668, 17679, 17643, 91376, 77918, 91239). The database reveals that all the captains had traded at Old Calabar for some time, some as long as twenty years. The English captains were almost certainly well known to one another. Parke and Lace, for instance, were partners on several voyages to Old Calabar before and after the massacre. See Eltis et al., eds., *Trans-Atlantic Slave Trade*, Unique Identity Numbers 91573, 91574, 91575, 91576, 91594, 91595.

11. Hall's testimony in Lambert, ed., *House of Commons Sessional Papers*, vol. 72, 537.

12. Forde, ed., *Efik Traders of Old Calabar*, 68–69.

13. PRO, KB 1/19/3, Mich. 1773, affidavit of William Floyd, Sept. 30, 1773.

14. Ancona Robin John to Charles Wesley, Aug. 17, 1774, in the Charles Wesley Papers, John Rylands Library, Manchester, Eng.; *Arminian Magazine*, Feb. 1783, 98–99, March 1783, 151; Clarkson, *History of the Rise, Progress, and Accomplishment of the Abolition of the African Slave Trade*, vol. 1, 305–310; Daryll Forde, ed., *Efik Traders of Old Calabar*, 68–69 (final quotation on p. 69); Lambert, ed., *House of Commons Sessional Papers*, vol. 73, 385–386.

15. Lambert, ed., *House of Commons Sessional Papers*, vol. 72, 515–517, 557.

16. Orrock Robin John to Marchant [Thomas] Jones, (undated, 1767?), King George to Marchant [Thomas] Jones (undated, 1767?), and Lace to Thomas Jones, Nov. 11, 1773, quoted in Lovejoy and David Richardson, "Letters of the Old Calabar Slave Trade, 1760–1789," 102 (first quotation), 103, 104, 108 (second quotation).

17. Colley quoted in Noah, *Old Calabar*, 19; Grandy King George to Mr. Ambrose Lace and Company (Jan. 13, 1773), quoted in Lovejoy and Richardson, "Letters of the Old Calabar Slave Trade," 104–105.

18. David Brion Davis, *The Problem of Slavery in the Age of Revolution, 1770–1823* (Ithaca, 1975), 41; Eltis et al., eds., *Trans-Atlantic Slave Trade*, Analysis, Summary (Any CAPTAIN = Lace, Any OWNER = Lace). On sharks see P. E. H. Hair, Adam Jones, and Robin Law, *Barbot on Guinea: The Writings of Jean Barbot on West Africa, 1678–1712*, 2 vols. (London, 1992), vol. 2, 732.

19. Lambert, ed., *House of Commons Sessional Papers*, vol. 72, 633–635.

20. Williams, *History of the Liverpool Privateers*, 541–542.

21. The acts are quoted in Ruth Paley, "After *Somerset:* Mansfield, Slavery and the Law in England, 1772–1830" (forthcoming). For additional information on the parliamentary hearings see Chapter 6.

22. Hall's testimony in Lambert, ed., *House of Commons Sessional Papers*, vol. 72, 556.

2. *"Nothing But Sivellety and Fare Trade"*

1. Grandy King George (to Ambrose Lace, undated, 1773?), reproduced in Lovejoy and Richardson, "Letters of the Old

Calabar Slave Trade," 106. The best overview of the slave trade in southeastern Nigeria remains Northrup, *Trade without Rulers*. On civility see David S. Shields, *Civil Tongues and Polite Behaviors in British America* (Chapel Hill, 1997).

2. On Efik adaptability and the rapid changes that accompanied the rise of the slave trade see E. O. Erim, "Cross-Cultural Contacts between the Efik and the Upper-Cross River Peoples, 1600–1900 A.D.," in S. O. Jaja, E. O. Erim, and Bassey W. Andah, eds., *Old Calabar Revisited* (Enugu, Nigeria, 1990), 172; Noah, *Old Calabar*, 26–27; A. J. H. Latham, *Old Calabar, 1600–1891: The Impact of the International Economy upon a Traditional Society* (Oxford, 1973), 13.

3. The Bight of Biafra, on the eastern bay of the Gulf of Guinea, extends approximately from the Niger River delta in southern Nigeria to northern Gabon. Old Calabar should not be confused with New Calabar or Elem Kalabari, another important slave port located north of Old Calabar in the Niger Delta.

4. Simmons, "Ethnographic Sketch," 3; Aye, *Old Calabar*, 23–24.

5. Hair, Jones, and Law, eds., *Barbot on Guinea*, vol. 2, 672, 677 (first quotation), 678, 701; G. I. Jones, "The Political Organization of Old Calabar," in Forde, ed., *Efik Traders*, 116–135; Nzewunwa, "Pre-colonial Nigeria," 31–32; Kannan K. Nair, *The Origins and Development of Efik Settlements in Southeastern Nigeria* (Athens, Ohio, 1975), 19–29.

6. Hair , Jones, and Law, eds., *Barbot on Guinea*, vol. 2, 549. On different means of enslavement see Northrup, *Trade without Rulers*, 65–80; Hope Masterson Waddell, *Twenty-Nine Years in the West Indies and Central Africa* (n.p., 1970), xxi, 315–319; Simmons, "Ethnographic Sketch," 7; Forde, ed., *Efik Traders*, 75, 134–135; Aye, *Old Calabar*, 88, 93–96; Herbert S. Klein, *The Atlantic Slave Trade* (Cambridge, Eng., 1999), 106–107, 117 (second quotation); George E. Brooks, *Landlords and Strangers: Ecol-*

ogy, *Society, and Trade in Western Africa, 1000–1630* (Boulder, 1992), 319; Ambrose Lace to Thomas Jones, Nov. 11, 1773 (second quotation), reproduced in Lovejoy and Richardson, "Letters of the Old Calabar Slave Trade," 107–108; Morley's testimony in Lambert, ed., *House of Commons Sessional Papers*, vol. 73, 154. On the role of slavery in the African political economy see Joseph C. Miller, *Way of Death: Merchant Capitalism and the Angolan Slave Trade, 1730–1830* (Madison, Wis., 1988), 40–70.

7. Northrup, *Trade without Rulers*, 16–17, 42; Lovejoy and Richardson, "Trust, Pawnship, and Atlantic History," 337–338; David Eltis, Paul E. Lovejoy, and David Richardson, "Slave-Trading Ports: Towards an Atlantic-Wide Perspective, 1676–1832," in Robin Law and Silke Strickrodt, eds., *Ports of the Slave Trade (Bights of Benin and Biafra)* (Sterling, Eng., 1999), 21–23; Latham, *Old Calabar*, 18–23; Klein, *Atlantic Slave Trade*, 62–64; Noah, *Old Calabar*, 5; Kenneth Morgan, *Bristol and the Atlantic Trade in the Eighteenth Century* (Cambridge, Eng., 1993), 138. The figures on the volume of the slave trade from Old Calabar are compiled from Eltis et al., eds., *Trans-Atlantic Slave Trade*. Since the database does not list every slave voyage, the numbers should be considered minimum estimates.

8. Northrup, *Trade without Rulers*, 89 (quotations); see also chaps. 1–6. Miller, *Way of Death*, 71–104. For general discussions of Old Calabar history see Aye, *Old Calabar;* Latham, *Old Calabar;* Noah, *Old Calabar;* Forde, ed., *Efik Traders*, 27–155; Lorena Walsh, *From Calabar to Carter's Grove: The History of a Virginia Slave Community* (Charlottesville, 1997), 67–80; Robin Law, *The Slave Coast of West Africa, 1550–1750: The Impact of the Atlantic Slave Trade on an African Society* (Oxford, 1991), chaps. 2–4; Kannan K. Nair, *Politics and Society in South Eastern Nigeria, 1841–1906* (London, 1972), 1–18.

9. Hair, Jones, and Law, *Barbot on Guinea*, vol.2, 674 (first

and second quotations); Morgan, *Bristol and the Atlantic Trade*, 135–136; Simmons, "Ethnographic Sketch," 6, 8; Simmons, "Notes," 68; Jones, "Political Organization," 124, 131; Lovejoy and Richardson, "Trust, Pawnship, and Atlantic History," 340–344; Bernard Martin and Mark Spurrell, eds., *The Journal of a Slave Trader (John Newton), 1750–1754* (London, 1962), 110 (third quotation). Contrast the trade at Old Calabar with the English factory system at Bance Island in Sierra Leone. See David Hancock, *Citizens of the World: London Merchants and the Integration of the British Atlantic Economy, 1735–1785* (Cambridge, Eng., 1995), 172–220. Stephen Behrendt found that British firms sometimes used their ships as "floating factories." They sent out experienced captains who paid the necessary comey and dashes (or gifts), and then purchased slaves for one or more ships. The firm then sent out additional ships over a period of months; these ships could load slaves more quickly and efficiently from the floating factories. His study begins in the late eighteenth century, but this practice may well have been a part of the earlier trade at Old Calabar. See Behrendt, "The British Slave Trade, 1785–1807: Volume, Profitability, and Mortality," (Ph.D. diss., University of Wisconsin, Madison, 1993), 117–118.

10. Similar and related English-based creole languages spread along the West African coast from Senegal to Nigeria and from there to the New World. See Ian F. Hancock, "A Provisional Comparison of the English-based Atlantic Creoles," *Sierra Leone Language Review*, 8 (1969), 7–72; Hancock, "Gullah and Barbadian: Origins and Relationships," *American Speech*, 55 (1980), 17–35; Lorenzo Dow Turner, *Africanisms in the Gullah Dialect* (1949; rpt. Ann Arbor, 1973); E. Tonkin, "Some Coastal Pidgins in West Africa," in Edwin Ardener, ed., *Social Anthropology and Language* (London, 1973), 129–155. The term "pidgin" must be used with care. A pidgin is a simplified version of some lan-

guage, often containing features from other languages as well. Associated with European expansion and colonialism, a pidgin is used solely as a trade language and does not have native speakers. In this context, creolization, a complex process of sociolinguistic change, is the creation of a new language. It occurs when a first-generation pidgin becomes the native language of a generation of speakers, and it is marked by an expanding vocabulary that goes beyond the necessities of trade, and by a more complex grammatical structure. Hancock uses the term "Atlantic Creoles" carefully to denote languages that were once pidgins but that subsequently became native languages, as was the case in Old Calabar. These trade languages emerged in West Africa in the sixteenth century and had made the transition to creole languages by the second half of the eighteenth century, as the letters from Efik merchants and the diary of Antera Duke make clear. For references to the Atlantic creole language of Old Calabar as pidgin English see Lovejoy and Richardson, "Letters of the Old Calabar Slave Trade" and "Trust, Pawnship, and Atlantic History," 341–342. On the debate surrounding pidgins and creoles see Derek Bickerton, "Pidgin and Creole Studies," *Annual Review of Anthropology*, 5 (1976), 169–193; Helen Thomas, *Romanticism and Slave Narratives: Transatlantic Testimonies* (Cambridge, Eng., 2000), 162–165.

11. Aye, *Old Calabar*, 86–88, 108–109; Latham, *Old Calabar*, 27–28; Lovejoy and Richardson, "Trust, Pawnship, and Atlantic History," 339–346. On language and literacy see especially Lovejoy and Richardson, ibid., 341–342 ; Lovejoy and Richardson, "Letters of the Old Calabar Slave Trade," 89–115; Williams, *History of the Liverpool Privateers*, 543–553; and the remarkable diary of Antera Duke published in Chief Ukorebi U. Asuquo, "The Diary of Antera Duke of Old Calabar (1785–1788), *The Calabar Historical Journal*, 5 (1978): 32–42, and in Forde, ed.,

Efik Traders, 27–155; Hancock, *Citizens of the World*, 103 (third quotation); Lambert, ed., *House of Commons Sessional Papers*, vol. 72, 543 (first quotation), vol. 69, 49 (second quotation), 84–86 (remaining quotations). A nineteenth-century English merchant noted that in Old Calabar "many of the natives write English; an art first acquired by some of the traders' sons, who had visited England, and which they have had the sagacity to retain up to the present period. They have established schools and schoolmasters, for the purpose of instructing in this art the youths belonging to families of consequence." Captain John Adams, *Remarks on the Country Extending from Cape Palmas to the River Congo* (London, 1823), 144. The Efik's ready mastery of written English may have been encouraged by the fact that they had their own indigenous form of ideographic writing that was closely associated with Ngbe. See Robert Farris Thompson, *Flash of the Spirit: African and Afro-American Art and Philosophy* (New York, 1983), 227–268. Tradition in Old Calabar suggests that schools teaching English dated back perhaps to the seventeenth century, and a seventeenth-century writing slate in folio form that reputedly belonged to an Efuk ruler is still preserved. Ekei Essien Oku, *Kings and Chiefs of Old Calabar*, 12. The Efik were not the only slave traders who sent their children to Europe to be educated. For French examples see Robert Harms, *The Diligent: A Voyage through the Worlds of the Slave Trade* (New York, 2002), 18.

12. Forde, ed., *Efik Traders*, 32 (first quotation), 51 (second quotation); Willm Earle to Duke Abashy, Feb. 10, 1761, and King George to Marchant [Thomas] Jones (undated, 1769?), in Lovejoy and Richardson, "Letters of the Old Calabar Slave Trade," 99 (third quotation), 103 (fourth and fifth quotations).

13. Lambert, ed., *House of Commons Sessional Papers*, vol. 72, 84–86) (first quotation). English traders also referred to the Afri-

can traders as gentlemen in correspondence between themselves (see Williams, *History of the Liverpool Privateers,* 533). On holiday parties see Asuquo, "Diary," 49. On using English joiners to build houses see Forde, ed., *Efik Traders,* 37, 41, 58; Latham, *Old Calabar,* 27–28. On consumption goods and the efforts of English merchants to cater to African demands see David Richardson, "West African Consumption Patterns and Their Influence on the Eighteenth-Century English Slave Trade," in Henry A. Gemery and Jan S. Hogendorn, eds., *The Uncommon Market: Essays on the Atlantic Slave Trade* (New York, 1979), 303–330. On trust, pawnship, and the relationship between Efik and English traders see Lovejoy and Richardson, "Trust, Pawnship, and Atlantic History," 339–344, and Lovejoy and Richardson, "The Business of Slaving: Pawnship in Western Africa, c. 1600–1810," *Journal of African History,* 42 (Jan. 2001), 67–90. On sons and daughters of traders as pawns see Hall's testimony in Lambert, ed., *House of Commons Sessional Papers,* vol. 72, 515. Williams, *History of the Liverpool Privateers,* 545 (second quotation). Richard Jackson of Liverpool was captain of the *Integrity* and traded in Old Calabar in 1773. See Eltis et al., eds., *Trans-Atlantic Slave Trade,* Unique Identity Number 91458; Martin and Spurell, *Journal of a Slave Trader,* 39, 42.

14. Herbert Klein noted that the Efik's long reliance on kidnapping and raiding as a source of slaves is a "highly unusual" situation. Klein, *Atlantic Slave Trade,* 116–121 (first quotation on p. 119); Hall's testimony in Lambert, ed., *House of Commons Sessional Papers,* vol. 72, 514–515, 525, 635, vol. 69, 49 (second quotation); Paul E. Lovejoy and Jan S. Hogendorn, "Slave Marketing in West Africa," in Gemery and Hogendorn, eds., *Uncommon Market,* 227; Richard Olaniyan, "The Atlantic Slave Trade," in Olaniyan, ed., *Nigerian History and Culture,* 118–119; Lovejoy and Richardson, "Trust, Pawnship, and Atlantic History," 339;

Martin A. Klein, "The Slave Trade and Decentralized Societies," *Journal of African History*, 42 (Jan. 2001), 49–66; Elisabeth Isichei, *The History of the Igbo People* (London, 1976); A. E. Afigbo, *The Igbo and Their Neighbors*, (Ibadan, Nigeria, 1987); J. No. Oriji, *Traditions of Igbo Origin: A Study of Pre-Colonial Population Movements in Africa* (New York, 1994); J. Okoro Ijoma and O. N. Njoku, "High Point of Igbo Civilization: The Arochukwu Period," in A. E. Afigbo, ed., *Groundwork of Igbo History* (Lagos, Nigeria, 1991), 198–312; Felicia Ekejiuba, "High Points of Igbo Civilization: The Arochukwu Period, A Sociologist's View," in Afigbo, ed., *Groundwork*, 313–332; K. Onwuka Dike, *The Aro of South-eastern Nigeria, 1650–1980: A Study of Socio-economic Formation and Transformation in Nigeria* (Ibadan, Nigeria, 1990).

15. Hair, Jones, and Law, eds., *Barbot on Guinea*, vol. 2, 680–681; Lambert, ed., *House of Commons Sessional Papers*, vol. 69.

16. Lambert, ed., *House of Commons Sessional Papers*, vol. 69, 124–137 (quotation on p. 130). Clarkson reported a case where eleven sailors deserted at Bonny, a major slave-trading port in what is now Nigeria, rather than remain with an abusive captain. Clarkson, *History of the Abolition of the Slave Trade*, 338–339.

17. Lambert, ed., *House of Commons Sessional Papers*, vol. 72, 521, 522, vol. 73, 124–137. Captain George Colley made several slave-trading voyages to Africa between 1758 and 1769. He is known to have purchased 2,059 slaves there, of whom 1,775 survived the Middle Passage to be sold in America. The *Latham*, owned and commanded by Colley, left Liverpool on April 20, 1766. Colley purchased 381 slaves on the African coast; 308 were sold in Barbados and Grenada. He returned to Old Calabar with the *Latham* in 1768; there his ship was cut off from the shore by hostile African traders at Old Calabar, but escaped from them and completed its voyage to America. It was Colley's last re-

corded voyage. Parker's adventures at sea were not over either. He sailed around the world with Captain James Cook as a boatswain's mate on board the *Endeavour*. Information about Colley's record can be found in Eltis et al., eds., *Trans-Atlantic Slave Trade* (see records 91292 and 91293 for the *Latham*).

18. Lambert, ed., *House of Commons Sessional Papers*, vol. 72, 132–133, vol. 73, 586. Williams, *History of the Liverpool Privateers*, 486 (quotation).

19. G. I. Jones, "The Political Organization of Old Calabar" in Forde, ed., *Efik Traders*, 123–124; Klein, *Atlantic Slave Trade*, 116, 119; Lovejoy and Richardson, "Trust, Pawnship, and Atlantic History," 340–341, 348; Olaniyan, "Atlantic Slave Trade," 116–120; Nair, *Politics and Society in South Eastern Nigeria*, 1–14; Miller, *Way of Death*, 94–104 (quotation on p. 94); Latham, "Currency, Credit, and Capitalism on the Cross River in the Pre-Colonial Era," *Journal of African History*, 12 (1971), 604.

20. Jones, "Political Organization," 134–135; Lambert, ed., *House of Commons Sessional Papers*, vol. 73, 152–153; Waddell, *Twenty-Nine Years*, 318–321; Nzewunwa, "Pre-colonial Nigeria," 29–32; Miller, *Way of Death*, 101–103, 676.

21. Northrup, *Trade without Rulers*, 180; Waddell, *Twenty-Nine Years*, 320; Williams, *History of the Liverpool Privateers*, 534; Miller, *Way of Death*, 174–175; Latham, "Currency, Credit, and Capitalism," 604; Hair, Jones, and Law, eds., *Barbot on Guinea*, vol. 2, 677 (quotation), 680–681, 707, 790–791. For other examples of the trade in provisions see the diary of Antera Duke in Forde, ed., *Efik Traders*, 28, 40–41.

22. Thompson, *Flash of the Spirit*, 239–240. Lovejoy and Richardson date the introduction of Ekpe to the second half of the seventeenth century. See Lovejoy and Richardson, "Trust, Pawnship, and Atlantic History," 347. Nair, *Politics and Society*, 14–20.

23. Forde, ed., *Efik Traders*, 137–148; Latham, "Currency, Credit, and Capitalism," 2–13, 25–27, 31–41; Noah, *Old Calabar*, 1–15, 20–27; Northrup, *Trade without Rulers*, 108–110; Lovejoy and Richardson, "Trust, Pawnship, and Atlantic History," 346–349.

24. Forde, ed., *Efik Traders*, vii, 13–14, 59, 137–148 (Antera Duke quoted on pp. 29–30 [first quotation], 49 [second quotation]); Latham, "Currency, Credit, and Capitalism," 2–13, 25–27, 31–41; Noah, *Old Calabar*, 1–15, 20–27; Lovejoy and Richardson, "Trust, Pawnship, and Atlantic History," 346–349; Nair, *Politics and Society*, 24.

25. Waddell, *Twenty-Nine Years*, 265–266; Noah, *Old Calabar*, 27–32; Thompson, *Flash of the Spirit*, 244–268; Simon Ottenberg and Linda Knudsen, "Leopard Society Masquerades: Symbolism and Diffusion," *African Arts*, 18 (1985), 37–44, 93–95, 103–104; Lovejoy and Richardson, "Trust, Pawnship, and Atlantic History," 348.

26. The Efik eight-day week consisted of four day names repeated in cycles differentiated by the adjectives *awka* (big) and *ekpri* (small). Personal names were often derived from these day names. Forde, ed., *Efik Traders*, 72.

27. Forde, ed., *Efik Traders*, 19–21 (first quotation on p. 19), 43, 71, 77; Noah, *Old Calabar*, 39–44; Waddell, *Twenty-Nine Years*, 380–382.

28. Rosalind I. J. Hackett, *Religion in Calabar: The Religious Life and History of a Nigerian Town* (Berlin, 1989), 27–34; Waddell, *Twenty-Nine Years*, 328–329; Forde, ed., *Efik Traders*, 19–20.

29. Nair, *Politics and Society*, 27–28; Waddell, *Twenty-Nine Years*, 310; Noah, *Old Calabar*, 70–72; Lovejoy and Richardson, "Trust, Pawnship, and Atlantic History," 347–349.

30. Grandy King George to Mr. Ambrose Lace, Jan. 13, 1773,

in Lovejoy and Richardson, "Letters of the Old Calabar Slave Trade," 104–111; Lovejoy and Richardson, "Trust, Pawnship, and Atlantic History," 347–348.

31. D. Simmons, "Ethnographic Sketch," 16–19; Jones, "Political Organization of Old Calabar," 135–148; Noah, *Old Calabar*, 70–71; Lovejoy and Richardson, "Trust, Pawnship, and Atlantic History," 336, 343, 353–355; Klein, *Atlantic Slave Trade*, 117–119. Atkins quoted in Harms, *The Diligent*, 123. For other examples of attacks on European merchants or their forts and trading lodges or European raids and kidnapping see Harms, *The Diligent*, 146–147, 151, 204, 220.

32. Forde, ed., *Efik Traders*, vii, 13–14; Latham, *Old Calabar*, 2–13, 25–27, 31–41; Noah, *Old Calabar*, 1–15, 20–27; Lovejoy and Richardson, "Trust, Pawnship, and Atlantic History," 346–349; Klein, *Atlantic Slave Trade*, 106–114.

3. *"This Deplorable Condition"*

1. At least three letters survive from relatives in Old Calabar that mention Little Ephraim and Ancona, two from Ephraim Robin John and one from Orrock Robin John, all addressed to Thomas Jones of Bristol. See Orrock Robin John to "Marchant Jones" (undated, 1768–69?); Ephraim Robin John to "Marchant Jones," June 16, 1769; and King George [Ephraim Robin John] to "Marchant Jones" (undated, 1769?) in James Rogers Papers, PRO, C 107/1. The letters suggest that the Robin Johns' relatives in Old Calabar did not know for sure which captain had abducted the young men. These letters are reproduced in Lovejoy and Richardson, "Letters of the Old Calabar Slave Trade," 102–103.

2. Stanley M. Elkins discussed the "shock and detachment" that captives experienced and the ensuing negative effects on them, a thesis that generated a heated debate among historians.

See Elkins, *Slavery: A Problem in American Institutional and Intellectual Life* (Chicago, 1959), and Ann J. Lane, ed., *The Debate over Slavery: Stanley Elkins and His Critics* (Urbana, Ill., 1971). The literature on the Atlantic slave trade is vast. For a recent overview of the literature see the bibliographic essay in Klein, *Atlantic Slave Trade*, 213–224.

3. Lambert, ed., *House of Commons Sessional Papers*, vol. 72, 540–543, 525.

4. Hair, Jones, and Law, eds., *Barbot on Guinea*, vol. 2, 550 (quotation); Miller, *Way of Death*, 413.

5. For examples of English slavers' attempts to return captives to Old Calabar see Willm Earle to Duke Abashy, Feb. 10, 1761; Grandy King George to Ambrose Lace, Jan. 13, 1773; Ambrose Lace to Thomas Jones, Nov. 11, 1773, in Lovejoy and Richardson, "Letters of the Old Calabar Slave Trade," 107–108.

6. William Earle to Duke Abashy, Feb. 10, 1761, in Lovejoy and Richardson, ed., "Letters of the Old Calabar Slave Trade," 99; Ambrose Lace to Thomas Jones in Williams, *History of the Liverpool Privateers*, 541–542.

7. Eltis et al., eds., *Trans-Atlantic Slave Trade*, Unique Identity Number 17668. The average tonnage of ships from Bristol to Africa was 120 tons during the period from 1764 to 1775. Morgan, *Bristol and the Atlantic Trade*, 44. For further information on slave ships and mortality rates see Walter E. Minchinton, "Characteristics of British Slaving Vessels, 1698–1775," *Journal of Interdisciplinary History*, 20 (Summer 1989), 53–81; Joseph C. Miller, "Mortality in the Eighteenth-Century Atlantic Slave Trade," *Journal of Interdisciplinary History*, 11 (Winter 1981), 385–423; Charles Garland and Herbert S. Klein, "The Allotment of Space for Slaves Aboard Eighteenth-Century British Slave Ships," *William and Mary Quarterly*, 3rd ser., 42 (April 1985), 238–248; Klein, *Atlantic Slave Trade*, 131–150. The death rate on

the *Duke of York*'s first recorded voyage, in 1764 under the command of a different captain, was 19.1 percent. Eltis et al., eds., *Trans-Atlantic Slave Trade*, Unique Identity Number 17583. Williams, *History of the Liverpool Privateers*, 486–487 (quotation). On the high death rate from the Bight of Biafra see Behrendt, "The British Slave Trade," 172, 176, 187, 210–211 (n. 51).

8. Williams, *History of the Liverpool Privateers*, 535 (first and second quotations); "Some Particulars of a Voyage to Guinea by James Arnold" in Lambert, ed., *House of Commons Sessional Papers*, vol. 69, Part 1, p. 50; John Ashley Hall's testimony, 514, 518–519 (third quotation on p. 518), 530; Hair, Jones, and Law, eds., *Barbot on Guinea*, vol. 2, 775 (fourth quotation), 732; David Richardson, "Shipboard Revolts, African Authority, and the Atlantic Slave Trade," *William and Mary Quarterly*, 3rd ser., 58 (Jan. 2001), 70–92; Harms, *The Diligent*, 262.

9. Lambert, ed., *House of Commons Sessional Papers*, vol. 73, Parker's testimony, 122–123, 127–128; Millar's testimony, 387–88 (second quotation); Morley's testimony, 158–159; Hair, Jones, and Law, eds., *Barbot on Guinea*, vol. 2, 558 (third quotation), 674 (first quotation); Clarkson, *History of the Rise, Progress, and Accomplishment of the Abolition of the African Slave Trade*, vol. 1, 375–377; Miller, *Way of Death*, 412, 420, 427; Harms, *The Diligent*, 261–262.

10. Lambert, ed., *House of Commons Sessional Papers*, vol. 72, Hall's testimony, 519 (first and second quotations), 547; Williams, *History of the Liverpool Privateers*, 475.

11. Lambert, ed., *House of Commons Sessional Papers*, vol. 72, Hall's testimony, 519 (first quotation), 547; Morley's testimony, 158; Williams, *History of the Liverpool Privateers*, 487 (second quotation).

12. Parker's testimony, 127.

13. Morley's testimony, 150 (first quotation), 160–161 (second

and third quotations); Klein, *Atlantic Slave Trade*, 84, 150–153. A boatswain served as foreman of the crew and maintained the rigging and the sails, and supervised the stores. The gunner was responsible for maintaining the armaments. Chief mates were skilled navigators. Second mates were responsible for keeping discipline among the crew and working the ship. For descriptions of the duties of crewmen see Ralph Davis, *The Rise of the English Shipping Industry in the Seventeenth and Eighteenth Centuries* (London, 1962), 110–113, 122.

14. C. M. MacInnes, *Bristol and the Slave Trade* (Bristol, 1963), 9; Morley's testimony, 162 (first quotation), 165–166; Parker's testimony, 134; Hall's testimony, 520–521 (second quotation), 522 (third quotation), 532–533; Davis, *Rise of the English Shipping Industry*, 142; Klein, *Atlantic Slave Trade*, 152–153.

15. Hall's testimony, 544, 545, 554 (quotation).

16. Ancona Robin John to Charles Wesley, Aug. 17, 1774. See Eltis et al., *Trans-Atlantic Slave Trade*, for the record of Bivins's voyage from Old Calabar to Dominica and the volume of the trade to Dominica. Thomas Atwood, *The History of the Island of Dominica* (1791; rpt. London, 1971), 72–82, 104, 216; Harms, *The Diligent*, 341–345; Julius S. Scott, "Crisscrossing Empires: Ships, Sailors, and Resistance in the Lesser Antilles in the Eighteenth Century," in Robert L. Paquette and Stanley L. Engerman, eds., *The Lesser Antilles in the Age of European Expansion* (Gainesville, 1996), 138–141; Lexxon Honychurch, "Slave Valley, Peasant Ridges: Topography, Colour and Land Settlement on Dominica," at *http://www.uwichill.edu.bb/bnccde/dominica/conference/apers/Honeychurch.html*, 2 (quotation).

17. Morley's testimony, 158–160 (first and second quotations); MacInnes, *Bristol and the Slave Trade*, 15 (third and fourth quotations); Harms, *The Diligent*, 315 (fifth quotation).

18. Ancona Robin John to Charles Wesley, Aug. 17, 1774

(first quotation); Atwood, *History of the Island*, 208; Scott, "Crisscrossing Empires," 139–141; Berlin, "From Creole to African," 268 (second quotation); Hair, Jones, and Law, eds., *Barbot on Guinea*, vol. 2, 774.

19. Grandy King George praised Sharp in a 1773 letter as a "very good man," though he was unaware of Sharp's treatment of his relatives. Quoted in Williams, *History of the Liverpool Privateers*, 544. Scott, "Crisscrossing Empires," 139 (first quotation); *Arminian Magazine*, March 1783, 152; Ancona Robin John to Charles Wesley, Aug. 17, 1774 (second quotation). The article in the *Arminian Magazine*, based on the testimony of the Robin Johns, identified the captain only as "Capt. S.," master of a sloop that carried the men from Dominica to Virginia. The database in Eltis et al., eds., *Trans-Atlantic Slave Trade*, made his identification possible. Captain William Sharp left Liverpool in 1767, traded for slaves in Africa, and sold them in Dominica before sailing on to Virginia. The records indicate that he sold 103 slaves in Dominica. Not surprisingly, the records do not record the sale of the stolen Robin Johns. See Eltis et al., eds., *Trans-Atlantic Slave Trade*, Unique Identity Number 91357. For Sharp's other voyages to Dominica see Unique Identity Numbers 91463 and 91462.

20. *Virginia Gazette*, Purdie and Dixon, eds., May 2, 1766, Dec. 4, 1766, Dec. 18, 1766, Jan. 1, 1767, March 4, 1773; Rind, ed., Aug. 1, 1771; Ancona Robin John to Charles Wesley, Aug. 17, 1774 (quotation).

21. A 1793 Jamaica newspaper described "a negroman called *Jack*, who shipped himself on the coast, and was to return thither." He was described as "a yellow negro, of a very stout make, and spoke a good deal of English. Captain Jones was frequently heard to declare, he would sell Jack at the Caymans." *The Royal Gazette* (Kingston, Jamaica), March 9, 1793. Some

captains did enslave sailors. A 1757 advertisement in a Liverpool newspaper offered for sale "ONE Stout NEGRO young fellow, about 20 years of age, that has been employed for 12 months on board a ship, and is a very serviceable hand." Quoted in Williams, *History of the Liverpool Privateers*, 475. For the story of Amissa see *History of the Liverpool Privateers*, 563–564. Paul Gilroy, *The Black Atlantic: Modernity and Double Consciousness* (Cambridge, Mass., 1993), 12 (first quotation); W. Jeffrey Bolster, *Black Jacks: African-American Seamen in the Age of Sail* (Cambridge, Mass., 1997), 4, 17, 20, 21, 24, 27, 37 .

22. *Virginia Gazette*, Rind, ed., March 12, 1772 (second quotation); Ancona Robin John to Charles Wesley, Aug. 17, 1774.

23. The Robin Johns identified O'Neil as the ship's captain, but according to the *Trans-Alantic Slave Trade* database Jacob Patterson was first captain of the ship. It is likely that Patterson did not survive the journey. The death rate among the crew was high on the voyage. Of forty-one crewmen who embarked on the trip from Bristol, only thirteen were alive when the ship left Charleston. See Eltis et al., eds., *Trans-Atlantic Slave Trade*, Unique Identity Number 17807. Ancona Robin John to Charles Wesley, Aug. 17, 1774.

4. "We Were Free People"

1. For verification of the ship, O'Neil, and the 1773 voyage, see Eltis et al., eds., *Trans-Atlantic Slave Trade*, Unique Identity Number 17807. Boatmen were in an unusually good position to make their escape. It was also not unusual for shippers to assist them. See Philip Morgan, *Slave Counterpoint: Black Culture in the Eighteenth-Century Chesapeake and Lowcountry* (Chapel Hill, 1998), 340–341. *Virginia Gazette*, Purdie and Dixon, eds., Sept. 30, 1773 (first quotation). *Arminian Magazine*, 6 (March 1783),

152–153; Ancona Robin John to Charles Wesley, Aug. 17, 1774; Ephraim Robin John to Charles Wesley, Aug. 17, 1774.

2. Morgan, *Bristol and the Atlantic Trade*, 9.

3. Ibid., 130–132 (quotation on p. 131), 140–142.

4. Ephraim Robin John to Charles Wesley, Aug. 17, 1774 (quotation); Orrock Robin John to Thomas Jones (undated, 1767?) and Grandee Ephraim Robin John (Grandy King George) to Thomas Jones, June 16, 1769, reproduced in Lovejoy and Richardson, "Letters of the Old Calabar Slave Trade," 102–103.

5. For the records of the court case see 23 George II c. 31 s. 29; PRO, KB 1/19/3, Mich. 1773, affidavit Thomas Jones, Oct. 21, 1773.

6. Ephraim Robin John to Charles Wesley, Aug. 17, 1774 (first and second quotations); Lovejoy and Richardson, "Trust, Pawnship, and Atlantic History," 342 (third quotation); Williams, *History of the Liverpool Privateers*, 541–542 (remaining quotations). For other examples of Africans traveling to or educated in Europe with the help of traders, see Robin Law and Kristin Mann, "West Africa in the Atlantic Community: The Case of the Slave Coast," *William and Mary Quarterly*, 3rd ser., 56 (1999), 315–321; James Walvin, *Black and White: The Negro and English Society, 1555–1945* (London, 1973), 51; and "From the Delegates from Liverpool, in Answer to the Enquiry made by the Committee respecting the Natives of Africa who have been sent to England for Education," Lambert, ed., *House of Commons Sessional Papers*, vol. 69, Part 1, 84–86.

7. Grandy King George to Ambrose Lace (undated, 1770s), reproduced in Williams, *History of the Liverpool Privateers*, 545–546.

8. I am extremely grateful to Ruth Paley for sharing her expertise and her unpublished manuscript discussing the legal im-

plications of the Robin Johns' case. I am indebted to her for my understanding of the topic. Paley, "After *Somerset*."

9. Mansfield's ruling is cited in F. O. Shayllon, *Black Slaves in Britain* (London, 1974), 109–110.

10. Teresa Michaels, "'That Sole and Despotic Dominion': Slaves, Wives, and Game in Blackstone's Commentaries," *Eighteenth-Century Studies*, 27 (Winter 1993–94), 205 (first quotation); Eric Williams, "The Golden Age of the Slave System in Britain," *Journal of Negro History*, 25 (Jan. 1940), 103; Franklin, *The Works of Benjamin Franklin*, John Bigelow, ed. and comp., vol. 5 (New York, 1904), 356 (third quotation); Shyllon, *Black Slaves in Britain*, 165–176 (second quotation on p. 165); David Brion Davis, *The Problem of Slavery*, 476, 478. Mansfield's nephew, Sir John Lindsay, took a black woman prisoner off a Spanish vessel and brought her to England, where she bore him a son and a daughter. When the daughter, Dido Elizabeth Lindsay, was an infant, Mansfield took her into his home, where her presence raised several eyebrows. One visitor in 1779 reported that "she is neither handsome nor genteel—pert enough. . . . He [Mansfield] knows he has been reproached for shewing a fondness for her—I dare say not criminal." When the *Somerset* case came before Mansfield, one West Indian planter announced that Somerset would be freed, "for Lord Mansfield keeps a Black in his house which governs him and the whole family." Mansfield thought it necessary to confirm her freedom in his will, a move that may indicate he had doubts about the legality of slavery in England even after the *Somerset* case. Shyllon, *Black Slaves in Britain*, 14–15, 169; Gretchen Gerzina, *Black London: Life before Emancipation* (New Brunswick, N.J., 1995), 88–89.

11. PRO, KB 1/19/3, Mich. 1773, affidavit Thomas Jones, Oct. 21 and Sept. 18, 1773; Paley, "After *Somerset*."

12. Little Ephraim Robin John to Charles Wesley, Aug. 17,

1774. Dr. Paley observed that Mansfield's decision to bring the men before him in London indicates an unusual interest in the case. Communication from Dr. Paley to the author, June 8, 2001.

13. Williams, *History of the Liverpool Privateers*, 545 (first quotation); Ephraim Robin John to Charles Wesley, Aug. 17, 1774; *Arminian Magazine*, 6 (April 1783), 211; Julius S. Scott, "Afro-America Sailors and the International Communication Network: The Case of Newport Bowers," in Colin Howell and Richard J. Twomey, eds., *Jack Tar in History: Essays in the History of Maritime Life and Labour* (Fredericton, New Brunswick, 1991), 38, 52. Southern planters watched and discussed the *Somerset* case, which meant, of course, that slaves quickly learned of its implications. See, for example, Jeffrey Robert Young, *Domesticating Slavery: The Master Class in Georgia and South Carolina, 1670–1837* (Chapel Hill, 1999), 71, and Morgan, *Slave Counterpoint*, 246, 461.

14. Thomas Clarkson, *The Substance of the Evidence of Sundry Persons on the Slave Trade . . .* (London, 1789), pp. 6–11 (quotation). Paley, "After *Somerset*."

15. Paley, "After *Somerset.*" (fourth quotation). Grandy King George to Thomas Jones (undated, 1767?), reproduced in Lovejoy and Richardson, "Letters of the Old Calabar Slave Trade," 103 (first quotation); PRO, KB 1/19/3, Mich. 1773, affidavit Thomas Jones, Oct. 3, 1773 (second and third quotations).

16. Paley, "After *Somerset*" (first quotation); Shyllon, *Black Slaves*, 44–45, n. 1 (second quotation), 50–54 (third and fourth quotations on p. 52, fifth quotation on p. 53); Davis, *The Problem of Slavery*, 488, 497.

17. Paley, "After *Somerset*." Orrock Robin John offered Thomas Jones three slaves if he returned lost family members. See Orrock Robin John to Thomas Jones (undated, 1767?), re-

produced in Lovejoy and Richardson, "Letters of the Old Calabar Slave Trade," 102–103.

18. Paley, "After *Somerset.*" See PRO, KB 21/40, Mich. 1773.

5. *"A Very Blessed Time"*

1. Martin and Spurrel, eds., *The Journal of a Slave Trader,*
103.

2. David Brion Davis, *The Problem of Slavery in Western
Culture* (Ithaca, 1966), 206–211 (quotation on p. 211).

3. Edmund S. Morgan, *American Slavery, American Freedom:
The Ordeal of Colonial Virginia* (New York, 1975), 329–332 (first
quotation on p. 331); Sylvia R. Frey and Betty Wood, *Come
Shouting to Zion: African American Protestantism in the American
South and British Caribbean to 1830* (Chapel Hill, 1998), 67–72,
93–94, 98, 111–114, 136–137 (second quotation on p. 70); Win-
throp D. Jordan, *White over Black: American Attitudes toward the
Negro, 1550–1812* (Chapel Hill, 1968), chap. 5; James Walvin,
England, Slaves, and Freedom, 1776–1838 (London, 1986), 39
(third quotation); Morgan, *Slave Counterpoint,* 648–651, 656
(fourth quotation on p. 649); Shyllon, *Black Slaves in Britain,*
24–28.

4. Morgan, *Slave Counterpoint,* 427–434; Frey and Wood,
Come Shouting to Zion, 106–107, 152–153, 155.

5. Noah, *Old Calabar,* 41–42 (first quotation); Forde, ed.,
Efik Traders, 69 (second quotation).

6. Jordan, *White over Black,* 23–24.

7. Rhys Isaac, *The Transformation of Virginia, 1740–1790*
(Chapel Hill, 1982), 260–263 (quotation on p. 263).

8. Thomas, *Romanticism and Slave Narratives,* 167–271 (first
quotation on p. 182); Ephraim Robin John and Ancona Robin
Robin John to Sarah Wesley, undated (second quotation); Davis,

Slavery in Western Culture, 459–464 (third quotation on p. 462); *Arminian Magazine*, 6 (March 1783), 151 (fourth quotation). Other Africans employed the same strategy and attempted to force the English to recognize the gulf that separated their practices from their faith. James Albert Ukawsaw Gronniosaw, an enslaved prince and convert like the Robin Johns, made his way to England because he "entertained a notion that if I could get to *England* I should never more experience either cruelty or ingratitude, so that I was very desirous to get among Christians." What he found, of course, shocked and disappointed him; "I could scarcely believe it possible that the place where so many eminent Christians had lived and preached could abound with so much wickedness and deceit. I thought it worse than *Sodom*." Gronniosaw, *A Narrative of The Most Remarkable Particulars in the Life of James Albert Ukawsaw Gronniosaw, An African Prince, Written by Himself* (Newport, R.I., 1774), 31–33.

9. Kenneth Morgan, ed., "Methodist Testimonials for Bristol Collected by Charles Wesley in 1742," in Jonathan Barry and Kenneth Morgan, eds., *Reformation and Revival in Eighteenth-Century Bristol* (Bristol, 1994), 77–79 (first quotation on p. 78); Frederick C. Gill, *Charles Wesley: The First Methodist* (New York, 1964), 32–33, 197, 230 (second quotation); Charles Wesley Flint, *Charles Wesley and His Colleagues* (Washington, D.C., 1957), 25, 159–160.

10. Kenneth Morgan, *John Wesley and Bristol* (Bristol, 1990), 3.

11. Ancona Robin John to Charles Wesley, Aug. 5, 1774; Ephraim Robin John to Charles Wesley, Aug. 17, 1774; Charles Wesley to Mr. William Perronet, Jan. 23, 1774 (final quotation). Noah, *Old Calabar*, 41–42 (second quotation); Forde, ed., *Efik Traders*, 69, 71; Thompson, *Flash of the Spirit*, 230–244.

12. Ephraim Robin John to Charles Wesley, August 17, 1774; *Arminian Magazine* VI (April 1783), 211.

13. Ephraim Robin John and Ancona Robin John to Sarah Wesley, undated. On correspondence between English and Efik slave traders see Chapter 2 and Lovejoy and Richardson, "Trust, Pawnship, and Atlantic History," 343–344, and "Letters of the Old Calabar Slave Trade," 89–115.

14. John Telford, ed., *The Letters of the Rev. John Wesley, A.M.* (London, 1931), vol. 4, 225, vol. 5, 84 (first quotation) vol. 6, 92, 129, 133 (second and third quotations), vol. 8, 188; John Wesley, *The Works of John Wesley* (Grand Rapids, n.d.), vol. 4, 255.

15. Wylie Sypher, "The African Prince in London," *Journal of the History of Ideas*, 2 (April 1941), 237–247 (quotation on p. 244); Gerzina, *Black London*, 11–14; Wylie Sypher, *Guinea's Captive Kings: British Anti-Slavery Literature of the XVIIIth Century* (New York, 1969), 59, 166–167; Davis, *Slavery in Western Culture*, 472–482.

16. Frey and Wood, *Come Shouting to Zion*, 87–91 (first quotation on p. 90); John R. Tyson, ed., *Charles Wesley: A Reader* (Oxford, 1989), 77–78 (second quotation).

17. Wesley, *Works of John Wesley*, vol. 2, 433, 464 (first quotation), vol. 6, 345 (fourth quotation). In 1786 Wesley baptized a "young negro" in Bristol. Warren Thomas Smith, *John Wesley and Slavery* (Nashville, Tenn., 1986), 58–59 (second and third quotations), 60–62, 65–66, 74, 76–89. Benezet quoted in Roger Anstey, *The Atlantic Slave Trade and Abolition, 1760–1810* (Atlantic Highlands, N.J., 1975), 240. Walvin, *England, Slaves, and Freedom*, 38–40, 52–55. Wesley read Benezet's *Some Historical Account of Guinea* (1771); Benezet to Sharp, Nov. 18, 1774 (Sharp Papers, Gloustershire Record Office, Gloucester, Eng.). Wes-

ley's letter to Benezet does not survive, but Benezet makes reference to it in his letter to Sharp.

18. Wesley, *Thoughts upon Slavery* (1774; rpt. New York, n.d.), 3 (first quotation), 6 (second and third quotations), 7 (fourth and fifth quotations), 18 (sixth quotation); Smith, *John Wesley and Slavery*, 90–103; Davis, *Slavery in Western Culture*, 382–390 (final quotation on p. 382); Anstey, *Atlantic Slave Trade*, 240.

19. Smith, *John Wesley and Slavery*, 60 (first quotation); Ephraim Robin John to Charles Wesley, Aug. 17, 1774 (second quotation); Wesley, *Thoughts upon Slavery*, 10–11, 20.

20. Ancona Robin John to Charles Wesley, Aug. 17, 1774.

6. *"We Go Home to Old Calabar"*

1. Ephraim Robin John to Charles Wesley, Aug. 17, 1774 (first quotation); Little Ephraim and Ancona Robin John to Charles Wesley, Feb. 18, 1774 (second quotation). Eltis et al., eds., *Trans-Atlantic Slave Trade*, Unique Identity Numbers 17671, 17729, 17860.

2. Boa Vista, the easternmost island of the Cape Verde archipelago closest to the African coast, is almost flat and covered with sand dunes. For a description see the Cape Verde website: *http://www.capeverde.co.uk/boavista.html*. Little Ephraim and Ancona Robin John to Charles Wesley (undated report of shipwreck). The wreck of the ship is confirmed in Eltis et al., eds., *Trans-Atlantic Slave Trade*, Unique Identity Number 17860. Elizabeth Johnson to Charles Wesley, June 16, 1774 (first, second, third, and fourth quotations).

3. Elizabeth Johnson to Charles Wesley, June 16, 1774 (first, second, third, and forth quotations); *Arminian Magazine* VI (April 1783), 211.

4. Elizabeth Johnson to Charles Wesley, June 16, Aug. 27, 1774; Little Ephraim Robin John to Charles Wesley, Aug. 27, 1774 (postscript).

5. Robin Law, "Legal and Illegal Enslavement in West Africa, in the Context of the Trans-Atlantic Slave Trade," unpublished paper presented at the Slavery, Enslavement, and Emancipation Conference held at Tel-Aviv University, March 2000, p. 1 (first quotation). I am grateful to Professor Law for sending me a copy of his paper. John Thornton, "African Political Ethics and the Slave Trade: Central African Dimensions," available at *http://muweb.millerville.edu/~winthrop/Thornton.html*, p. 1 (second and third quotations).

6. Ephraim Robin John to Charles Wesley, Sept. 26, 1774; Ancona Robin Robin John to Charles Wesley, Oct. 10, 1774. See Eltis et al., eds., *Trans-Atlantic Slave Trade*, Unique Identity Number 17851. The *Cato*, John Langdon, captain, was a ship of eighty tons. After delivering the Robin Johns, it took on 336 slaves in Calabar, 272 of whom survived the Middle Passage to be sold in Jamaica. Captain John Ashley Hall was in Old Calabar on the slave ship *Neptune* when Ephraim and Ancona returned. He heard their story firsthand and read copies of depositions they gave before winning their freedom in Bristol. See Lambert, ed., *House of Commons Sessional Papers*, vol. 72, 515–517, 527–528. The *Neptune* left London in January 1774 with Hall as second captain and traded for slaves on the coast of West Africa until it sailed for America later that year. The same ship left London for another voyage to Calabar in December 1774, which is probably when Hall encountered the Robin Johns. See Eltis et al., eds., *Trans-Atlantic Slave Trade*, Unique Identity Numbers 91935 and 77124.

7. Ann Chapman to Charles Wesley, Oct. 1774; Charles Wesley to the Rev. Perronet, Nov. 1, 1775 (first quotation). See

the letter from Ephraim Robin John to Captain Ambrose Lace of Dec. 5, 1775, spelling out details of the trade in slaves between them. Given the repetition of names among the Robin Johns, attribution is difficult. Williams, *History of the Liverpool Privateers*, 548–549; Asuquo, "Diary of Antera Duke," 34 (quotation); Aye, *Old Calabar*, 84. Another Calabar historian wrote, "Tradition has it that Otu Mbo and Afiong Mbo, children of the Obutong Chief, Mbo Otu who had died in the massacre in 1767, had been educated in England, and had on their return requested the King of their day to invite Missionaries right from 1790." Ekei Essien Oku, "Kings of Old Calabar" in S. O. Jaja, E. O. Erim, and B. W. Andah, eds., *Old Calabar Revisited* (Enugu, Nigeria, 1990), 39.

8. Luke Tyerman, *The Life and Times of the Rev. John Wesley, M.A., Founder of the Methodists* (New York, 1872), 272–273 (first quotation on p. 272, fourth quotation on p. 273); James McDonald, ed., *Memoirs of the Rev. Joseph Benson* (New York, 1823), vol. 1, 60 (second quotation); C. P. Groves, *The Planting of Christianity in Africa* (1954; rpt. London, 1964), vol. 2, 36–37; Ann Chapman to Charles Wesley, Oct. 1774 (third quotation).

9. Groves, *Planting of Christianity*, 37–38. One pupil refused instruction in Christianity and told Hope Waddell that "his father sent him to school to 'saby trade book,' and that he 'no want to saby God.'" Waddell, *Twenty-Nine Years*, 289, 251–253.

10. Coleridge quoted in Walvin, *England, Slaves, and Freedom*, 106 (third quotation); Clarkson, *The History of the Rise, Progress, and Accomplishment of the Abolition of the Slave Trade*, vol. 1, 255–256, 283 (first quotation), 286 (second quotation), 294 (fourth quotation).

11. Clarkson, *History of the Rise, Progress, and Accomplishment of the Abolition of the Slave Trade*, vol. 1, 304 (first quotation), 305 (second quotation), 310 (third quotation).

12. Ibid., vol, 1, 383–384. Clarkson identified Chaffers only by his surname, but the Cambridge Slave Trade Database makes it possible to identify him as Thomas Chaffers, who was captain of several slave ships sailing from Liverpool to West Africa in the 1750s and 1760s; see Eltis et al., eds., *Trans-Atlantic Slave Trade* (Any CAPTAIN = Chaffers). Lace had a slightly different recollection of the meal. See Lace's testimony in Lambert, ed., *House of Commons Sessional Papers*, vol. 72, 636.

13. Lace's testimony, vol. 72, 458–526; James Walvin, "The Public Campaign against Slavery in England, 1787–1834," in David Eltis and Walvin, eds., *The Abolition of the Atlantic Slave Trade: Origins and Effects in Europe, Africa, and the Americas* (Madison, Wisc., 1981), 63–67.

14. Davis, *Slavery in the Age of Revolution*, 422 (first quotation); Smith, *John Wesley and Slavery*, 104–120 (second quotation on p. 109); Clarkson, *History of the Rise, Progress, and Accomplishment of the Abolition of the Slave Trade*, vol. 1, 476 (third quotation).

15. Clarkson, *History of the Rise, Progress, and Accomplishment of the Abolition of the Slave Trade*, vol. 2, 2–11, 34–179 (first quotation on p. 175).

16. Ibid., vol. 2, 178 (first and second quotations), 186 (third and fourth quotations), 191–192 (fifth quotation on p. 192), 210–212; Davis, *Slavery in the Age of Revolution*, 422–443; Dale H. Porter, *The Abolition of the Slave Trade in England, 1784–1807* (n.p., 1970), 76–77; Anstey, *Atlantic Slave Trade*, 265; David Turley, *The Culture of English Antislavery, 1780–1860* (London, 1991), 60–64. See Lambert, ed., *House of Commons Sessional Papers*, vol. 2, Hall's testimony, 513–561; Parker testimony, 124–37 (especially pp. 132, 136; Millar's testimony, 385–388; Lace's testimony, 633–635.

17. Morgan, *Bristol and the Atlantic Trade*, 150–151 (first quo-

tation on p. 150). Wesley quoted in Smith, *John Wesley and Slavery,* 74–75.

18. Smith, *John Wesley and Slavery,* 118–119 (first quotation on p. 118, second on p. 119).

19. Millar's testimony, 385 (quotation).

20. Gilroy, *The Black Atlantic,* 16 (first quotation); Ephraim Robin John and Ancona Robin Robin John to Charles Wesley, Feb. 24, 1774 (second quotation).

Acknowledgments

I have accumulated many debts in completing this project, and would like to thank Ira Berlin, Seymour Drescher, Judith Lee Hunt, Herbert Klein, Igor Kopytoff, Jane Landers, Robin Law, Paul Lovejoy, Joseph Miller, Ruth Paley, Jane H. Pease and William H. Pease, and James Walvin for their assistance, suggestions and constructive criticisms. My special thanks go to Joyce Seltzer at Harvard University Press, whose support for the project has made it possible. I am grateful to the staff at the John Rylands Library, especially Dr. Peter Nockles, Dr. Dorothy Clayton, and Danielle Shields; and to Julie Richter, who assisted with research in Virginia. I would also like to thank the National Endowment for the Humanities and the Tulane Committee on Research Summer Fellowships for funding a portion of my research. Earlier versions of this essay were presented at the From Slavery to Freedom: Manumission in

the Atlantic World conference held at the College of
Charleston; as the Gottschalk Lecture in History at the
University of Louisville; at the Seventh Annual Meeting
of the Omohundro Institute of Early American History
and Culture, Glasgow, Scotland; at Citizens, Nations,
and Cultures: Transatlantic Perspectives, Maastricht
Center for Transatlantic Studies, Maastricht, Holland;
and at a Houston Area Southern Historians meeting at
Rice University, where commentators and members of
the audience provided much helpful feedback. Portions
of the manuscript appeared in "Two Princes of Calabar:
An Atlantic Odyssey from Slavery to Freedom," *William and Mary Quarterly*, 3rd ser., 59 (July 2002), 555–584.

Index